UNDERSTANDING VISUAL FORMS

Fundamentals of Two and Three Dimensional Design

Stewart Kranz and Robert Fisher

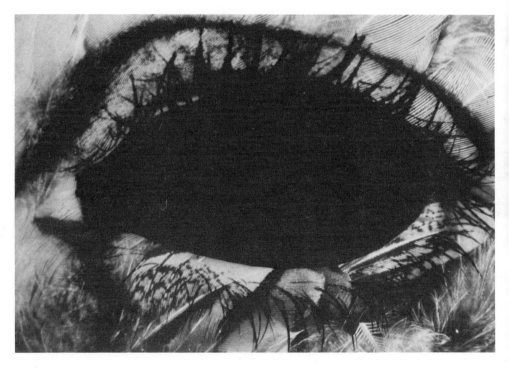

Based on
THE DESIGN CONTINUUM
Concept

 VAN NOSTRAND REINHOLD COMPANY
New York Cincinnati Toronto London Melbourne

Photography by Douglas Abbott and Robert Fisher

Also by the authors:
The Design Continuum (1966)
Science and Technology in the Arts (1974), by Stewart Kranz
Understanding Visual Forms (1976), color slides program

Copyright © 1976 by Litton Educational Publishing, Inc.
Library of Congress Catalog Card Number 75-16476
ISBN 0-442-24542-4 (paper)

Printed in the United States of America
Designed by Loudan Enterprises

Published in 1976 by Van Nostrand Reinhold Company
A Division of Litton Educational Publishing, Inc.
450 West 33rd Street
New York, NY 10001, U.S.A.

Van Nostrand Reinhold Limited
1410 Birchmount Road
Scarborough, Ontario M1P 2E7, Canada

Van Nostrand Reinhold Australia Pty. Ltd.
17 Queen Street
Mitcham, Victoria 3132, Australia

Van Nostrand Reinhold Company Ltd.
Molly Millars Lane
Wokingham, Berkshire, England

16 15 14 13 12 11 10 9 8 7 6 5 4 3 2 1

Library of Congress Cataloging in Publication Data

Kranz, Stewart.
    Understanding visual forms.

    1. Design. I. Fisher, Robert N., joint author.
II. Kranz, Stewart. The design continuum.
III. Title.
NK1520.K7 1976   745.4   75-16476
ISBN 0-442-24542-4

ACKNOWLEDGMENTS

We would like to express our appreciation to the many students whose work appears throughout this text. Their inventive solutions, curiosity, and enthusiasm during the past decade has been inspiring and rewarding. The continuing responsiveness of these students to the Design Continuum theory has both solidified and expanded our awareness of the value of the ideas contained herein leading up to this entirely new edition containing student solutions never having appeared previously. The projects shown were created in design classes from Syracuse University, Colorado State University, The University of Illinois, and The Pennsylvania State University.

We would also like to thank the Rare Book Library at the University of Illinois for permitting us to use the very unusual historical illustrations. The inclusion of such works adds depth and richness to our examples and opens up new avenues of visual exploration for the inquiring student.

Finally we wish to acknowledge the tremendous efforts and achievement of our photographer, Douglas Abbott, from Champaign, Illinois. Mr. Abbott combines the very rare capabilities of an accomplished musician with those of a very fine photographer. As a result, his vision is literary and poetic. His mastery of the many complications encountered during the original photography was awesome. To a considerable degree, Douglas was responsible for the development of the unique special effects used in the slides. These included precise matting, superimpositions, front and rear simultaneous projection and multiple projected images. His ability to balance and color correct all of the subtle forces at play in each image is to be applauded and we deeply appreciate his significant contribution to our work. Judith Vanderwall's willingness to plunge directly into this material also helped in the final preparation of the manuscript.

CONTENTS

INTRODUCTION

The vision of an astronaut floating in empty space made suddenly tangible a concept which lies at the core of our understanding of the visible world. The things we see, regardless of function, history, or process, are comprised of two opposing features, mass and space. The manner in which they relate in any given work establishes the primary characteristics of that work.

Our astronaut further illustrates the delicate balance between mass and space as they enact an unseen battle of forces in the changing forms of the world. A quarter inch of plasticized fabric is all that separates the astronaut from the astonishingly powerful negative pressure of the vacuum of space. The positive pressure in the space suit, which is created by the astronaut's life-support system, provides the precise atmosphere to counteract the negative force of space. It establishes and sustains his life. Without the pressure system inside, even the spacesuit, the thin skin between opposing forces, could not prevent the dispersion of the mass in his body outwards into the void.

Here, then, is the perfect metaphor for understanding our visual environment. Any and all objects are comprised of positive forces which suggest mass, negative forces which suggest space, and a surface which acts as an interface between the two forces. An abstract sphere, like a beach ball, represents a condition of balance between inside and outside. The equal pressure, distributing itself around the skin, or interface, creates the spherical form that we so quickly recognize. Similarly, a perfectly flat plane suggests a balance of forces. The skin of that plane, stretched taut in a painter's canvas, acts as an interface between the pressures of the outside world and the visual presence of the painter's inner world.

The interface, or surface, can give us information on the manner in which mass and space have resolved their differences. Perhaps it is a stand-off, as in the smooth, sleek surface of a jet aircraft. Or perhaps it is the fiery convulsions of the impressionist sculptures of Rosso or Rodin. The slightest breeze disturbs the surface of quiet pools of water, making visible the sensitive changing relationship between space and form. And, finally, there is the benign indifference of the highway billboard's huge, flat surface, intruding at worst on the psychological space of our thoughts.

Mass, space, and interface—with these terms we may describe most of the multitudinous forms we see. In order to study them best, we have applied a kind of systems analysis that enables us to describe each object not according to its color and size and shape but as a particular composition of mass and space. Taken together and in sequence, this series of relationships between mass and space creates a spiralling continuum that reveals, like a flower opening in time-lapse photographs, the intricacies of our visual world.

We call it the Design Continuum. It begins with a study of the concept of an interface in the existing flat planes of two-dimensional surfaces, from art objects such as drawings and paintings to natural surfaces like oil slicks on water or the patina on a pewter tray. Texture and relief evolve as the interface contorts and puckers, as if a pressure from inside had expanded the mass into space. Then, like mushrooms emerging from the rich soil of crumbling trees, forms begin to swell out of the interface. In these environmental relief forms, we explore the often unnoticed relationship between large isolated three-dimensional objects and the interface, or surface, upon which they are still firmly rooted. Two- and three-dimensional forms coexist in this way in country landscapes of broad fields and farm houses and architectural structures of a city or town. As forms separate from the plane we begin to see them as independent sculptures, first with bases, then without.

Finally, we return to the monolithic concept of a sphere floating alone in space, pristine in its resolution of forces, a perfect example of the balance of power between inner forces pushing outward and outer forces restraining them. As the outer forces grow stronger, the interface of the sphere begins to crinkle, pucker, and shrivel, and concave-convex forms appear that

7

bulge inwards and outwards like apples or pears or the human form. When the negative pressures of space become too strong, pieces of mass begin to disappear, like those mysterious "black holes" in our cosmos, where mass begins to contract and compress in on itself, perhaps in defense against the increasing negative momentum of space. Emptiness grows within the mass as the holes enlarge. Finally a balance is struck once again in three-dimensional planar forms, in which mass and interface act as a unit to articulate the flow of space, just as a thin sail catches the wind. The process goes on, with mass contracting in width now, condensing to linear three-dimensional forms like Calder mobiles tracing their ephemeral volumes in space. Unable to bear the strains of the pressures of space, mass chooses to maintain a "low profile," diminishing its interface to a construction of lines that can only suggest what was once a directive from its solid state.

And so it goes, plane to line to point to nothing. Space seems to be the victor. But all the while new suns form. There will be new worlds for future exploration. And our visual world becomes a little more comprehensible, its forms more clear and deliberate. Unbounded by historical data, purpose, scale, and even time, the sights we see take on a new meaning, one which allows for an infinity of application as broad in scope as space itself.

The following pages give further details about this changing relation between mass and space, in which forms flow into one another in an infinite series. We have put up signposts along the way, which we call stages in the design continuum, and we are going to explore each stage by approaching it from several different roads: the abstract concepts behind the forms, the contexts in which the forms appear in our world, and the projects and materials that students can use to create the forms.

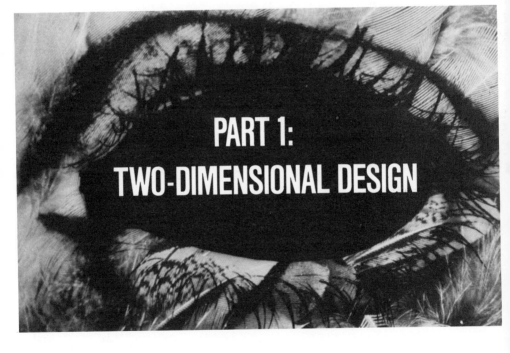

PART 1:
TWO-DIMENSIONAL DESIGN

TEXT TO STAGES 1-6, ROBERT FISHER

ANNOTATED CAPTIONS, STEWART KRANZ

STAGE 1:
FLAT TWO-DIMENSIONAL SURFACES

CONCEPT

As an abstraction, few concepts are more pregnant with possibilities than a two-dimensional surface. It is a surface with no reverse side and no thickness but with a length and width that are infinitely variable in proportion, shape, and size. In geometry we call this surface a plane. In our design continuum we describe it as a surface of unknown mass that interacts with space in essentially the same way at every point. It is a platform for the exploration of points, line, shape, color, repetition, pattern, proportion, figure and background, light and shade. It is an essential feature of the printed word, the printmaker's gravure, the oil painter's canvas, the medium of photography, the design of textiles, to name just a few examples.

When creating in this flat world that never gets off the ground, so to speak, a strange thing occurs. Deny yourself even the slightest sense of the illusion of space; restrict your vision to those elements and ideas which rest firmly at the surface of a plane; control your desire to move into or out from that surface. And an astonishing thing happens. You have so many possibilities open to you that your only guide is your imagination, your vision, and the examples of countless others whose disciplined exploration of the flat two-dimensional surface has gone before.

CONTEXT

Open this book to any page. From the layout, to the legibility and spacing of the type, to the proportions and relationships of the illustrations, book design is totally expressed on a flat surface. Medieval manuscripts and comic books, billboards and wallpaper, butterfly wings and prehistoric cave drawings, each reveal their ideas in two dimensions. Some of the most expressive art has deliberately ignored three-dimensional perspective—the disquieting sketches of Goya, the diagrams of DaVinci, the doodles of Miro or Klee or Picasso. In the hands of such artists, the surface boundaries of a flat plane have been made to mirror man's innermost thoughts.

Look at flat pattern in Nature. Is there no limit to the design of insect wings, the colorations of flower petals, leaves in the fall, the patchwork of farmland viewed from a passing jet? Or walk down a street, anytown, anywhere, looking at the patterns from the hand of man. Look at the stains on the sidewalk, scrawls on the walls, ads that scream out from windows, signs of our times. Or flip on the television screen and explore the spaces between channels, those test patterns and distortions of color and form, grainy pulses of light—impressionism and expressionism at the turn of a dial.

One cannot ever close one's eyes to the modes of flat expression because, when they are closed, optical fields of geometric forms arise out of nowhere, organic reminders of the human body and the human being as an ultimate source of ideas and expression.

APPROACHES AND MATERIALS

Get the point. Connect the dots. Make constellations of stars. Maximize the minimal. "Less is more."

Linear thought. How can you make a line? Think line. Thickness and thinness, smooth and agitated, rigid and curved, many and one. Random and rhythmic, drawn and scraped, scratched and etched, taped and tooled.

Shape up. Extend the lines into themselves and watch them become squares and circles, rocks and squiggles, blobs and boxes. Large, small, many, few, isolated, concentric, repeated over and over.

11

What is the value of it? Light, gray, dark. Everything light, everything dark, some things light, others dark. Rhythmical values out of dots, out of lines, changing patterns. Study camouflage. Find the true value of a work of art. Make it black and white. Black, white, and gray.

Figure and ground. One on the other, one in the other. The shapes between shapes. Space as shape.

Color wheeling and dealing. Same color, light and dark. One color many shapes, different values. One color, shapes repeated, different values. Complementary relationships, opposites expanding and vibrating. Optical art, pulsing surfaces of color, shape, line, dots. Now add value and repeat. Chroma, brightness and dullness, complements interceding when mixed up. Up and down the scale, from bright to dull, light to dark, red to orange to yellow to green to blue to violet. Prisms casting shadows of opposite hue.

Now put it all together with chalk, pencil, felt tip pen. Design a poster, a booklet, a sign or a symbol. Charcoal, brushes and ink, acrylic paint. Create a textile pattern, a fantasy, a gameboard. Cut paper, colored paper, newspaper, photographs, collographs, spatters of ink or paint, rubber cement, glue. Compete with butterflies for the wings of the year award. Snap a string on a board. Rule a line with a drawing pen. Scribe a circle with a compass, scratch a waxed board with an India inked surface. Invite a crowd of faces to look up at you from the surface of your work. Cut and paste shapes and colors. Watercolor, poster paints, spray paints, crayons. Weave a blanket of fall colors and shapes. Photography, solargrams and other direct images. Trace the sunlight as it casts its shadow through leaves.

CAPTION NOTES

The traditional surfaces for painting are simple planes. They do not project or recede or give the illusion of spatial depth. They connect with the observer's point of reference exactly the same way at every point on their surface. The following student examples play off geometric shapes and color so that they do not seem to project off the surface of the work.

Inside the image:

UNDERSTANDING VISUAL FORMS

FUNDAMENTALS OF TWO AND THREE DIMENSIONAL DESIGN

BY STEWART KRANZ AND ROBERT FISHER

PHOTOGRAPHY BY ROBERT FISHER AND DOUGLAS ABBOTT

VAN NOSTRAND REINHOLD COMPANY

NEW YORK CINCINNATI TORONTO LONDON MELBOURNE

B & W A-1a

This title image for the entire two-part *Understanding Visual Forms* introduces the basic format we have used throughout the set, in which a photograph of a human eye frames the visual area. The background of the Eye will be different in each stage of the continuum to provide a varying frame of reference for the student works. The rest of the images will be composites, and black-and-white illustrations of each of the components will also be reproduced.

Students of photography may be interested to know that the final visual image on the photos was created with an unusual technique of rear- and front-screened projection, using extensive mattes of positive and negative areas, as well as double, triple, and quadruple superimpositions. Later images will show this in more detail. To recreate these effects requires two, three, and four slide projectors. The surround and the Eye area both need black Kodalith mattes so the projectors projecting on the screen will not wash out the visual image in either the surround or the Eye area.

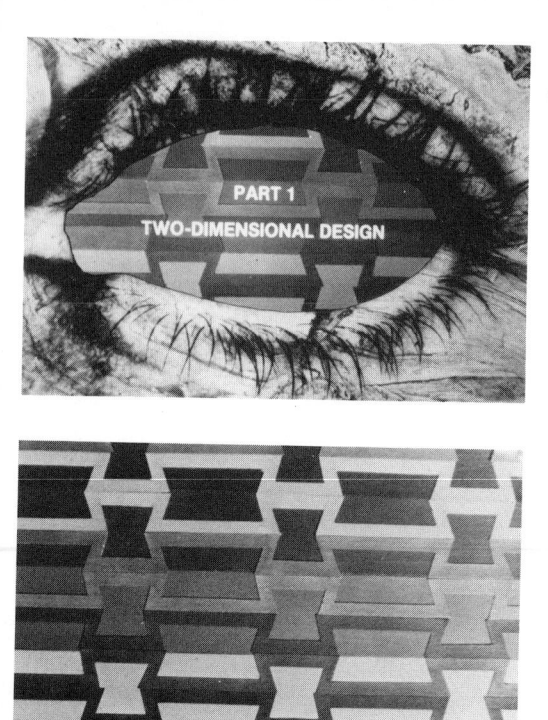

B & W A-2a, A-2b

This title image for *Part 1: Two Dimensional Design* uses a double projection, one for the eyelashes and eyebrows of the Eye, and the second for the very low relief in the surround area. Two projectors were used to create this effect. The central area is a segment of a blue and orange tempera rendering of a figure-ground relationship. As your eye moves from top to bottom of this student project you can see the blue functioning as ground and then becoming a positive area. The reverse is true in the orange, which changes slowly from a ground at the bottom to a figure at the top. The simple playoff between background and figure areas is expanded in the next six images, which form the illustrations proper for the first stage of our continuum.

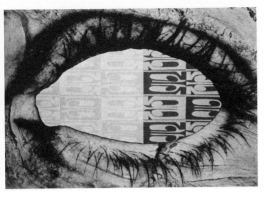

B&W A-3a, A-3b

Image A-3 has the same surround as our two introductory images. The slight relief of the surround and the Eye plays against the decorative two-dimensionality of the student project, which was achieved by changing the value and hue in a repeated tempera pattern.

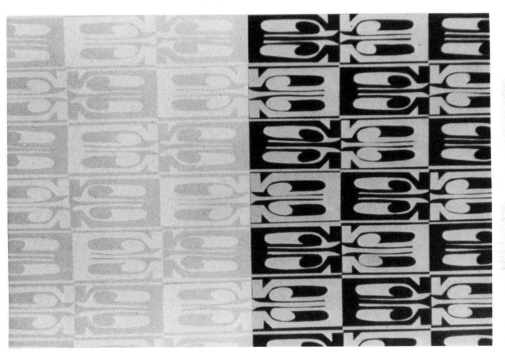

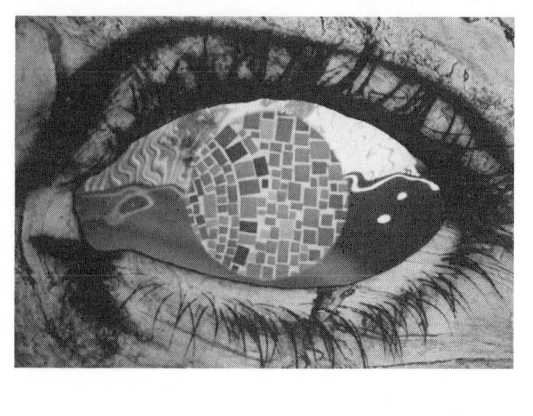

B&W A-4a, A-4b, A-4c

Here we see a student project super-imposed on a photograph from nature, the first of many such contrasts we will be making. In this composite, we are trying to show the analogy between the essential flatness of a mosaic and the pattern created by detergent floating on the surface of water. Although both are flat two-dimensional surfaces, the fluid lines of the water contrast strongly with the broken, geometric mosaic. The student project was created by acrylic, in varied values and chromas of one hue, painted on cut paper in units of varied sizes.

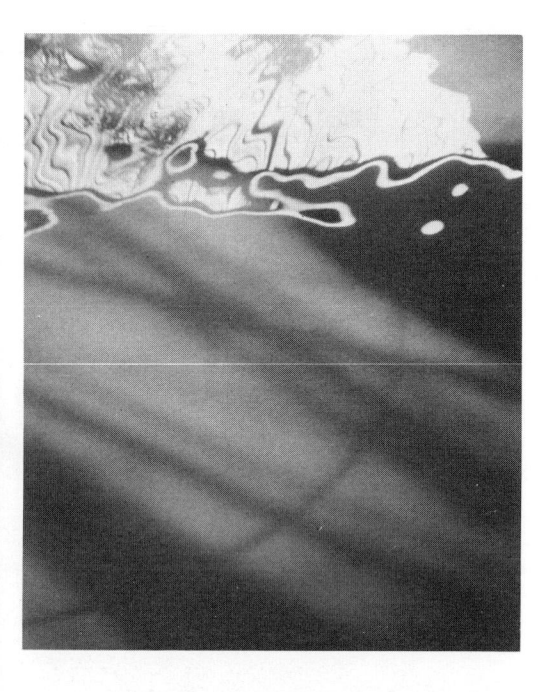

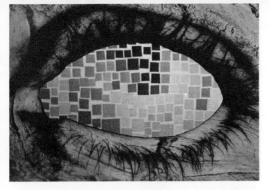

B&W A-5a, A-5b

This student project is a composition using the gray value scale with a single hue, in this case red-orange. The mosaic technique is an ideal method for preserving the visual flatness of the space because the breaks between the square tiles serve as an overall reminder, almost in the cubist tradition, that the surface is truly flat and not designed so the images project forward in space.

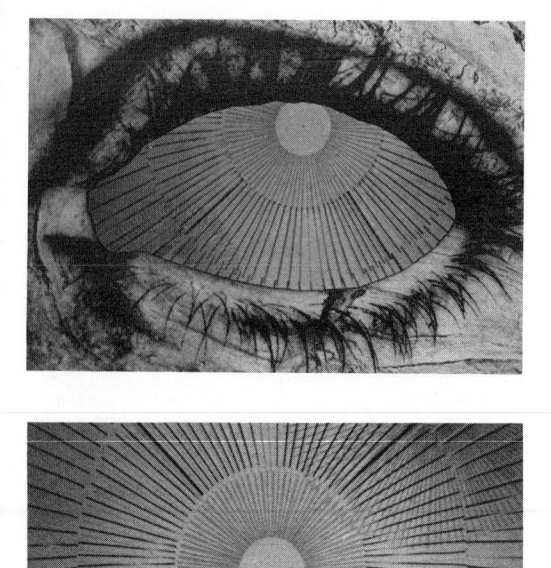

B & W A-6a, A-6b

This student project is an optical art exercise using a moiré-type pattern to allow the juxtaposition of complementary colors. Optical art such as this maintains the character of the two-dimensional surface on which the images are painted through a combination of color and physiological phenomena working together.

If you look closely at the image and the black-and-white illustration you can see how the two-dimensional effect is created here. A series of radiating lines are juxtaposed over two subordinate radiating areas of line. The sense of space is minimized by the breaks between the line areas in the concentric series of circles radiating out from the central sphere. This pattern, used with complementary colors forces a physiological reaction in the spectator's eye that is caused by the inability of the brain to accept such juxtaposed complements without considerable activity on the part of our visual apparatus to resolve the conflict between the two complementary colors.

In a sense, the whole principle of art is to create a visual overload, one in which the stimuli coming through the retina to the brain are more than the brain can comfortably interpret. In other words, optical art, by its very nature, helps to create the quality we are describing at this stage of the continuum.

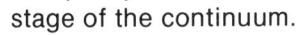

B & W A-7a, A-7b, A-7c

Here we have deliberately chosen two very different works of art in which a sensitive awareness on the part of the graphic artist allows a mixture of illustrative details with calligraphy. One example is 19th-century American folk art and the other is a medieval book illumination. A typeface with artistic embellishment has a psychological and physiological affinity to the flatness of the surface on which it is rendered, but could easily produce a spatial illusion. If the movement off or into the picture plane is accentuated by type, a disturbing conflict arises between the flat shapes of letters and numbers and their illusionary spatial characteristics. In both cases here, the essential flatness of the graphic surface is maintained. The black-and-white illustrations show full shots of the painted wood medicine wagon sign and the book illustration.

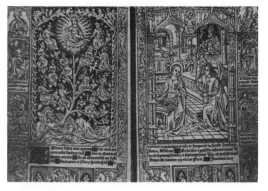

B&W A-8a, A-8b

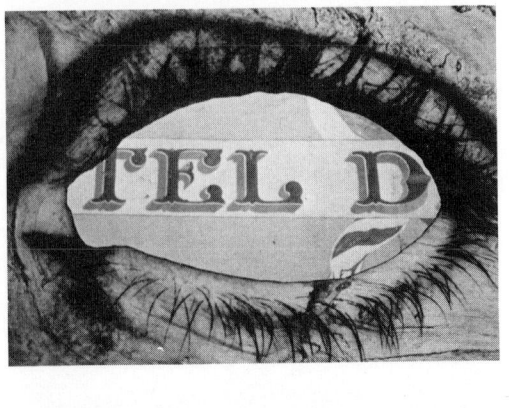

The handsome calligraphy in this example from a hotel facade in Georgetown, Colorado, is the exception which proves the rule. Relief painting and relief drawing have long utilized the idea of a shadow around a strong form to create a strong projection off the plane of the background into space. And in this example each letter in "tel" has a deep ochre drop shadow. Yet between the actual letter and the drop shadow, a thin line from the white background of this area of the sign intrudes. This simple device alone breaks what would otherwise be a very strong illusion of three dimensions. The sign painter, sensing the essential graphic character of the sign, breaks the sense of movement off the picture plane by bringing the white ground directly in at the very point at which a spatial illusion would be created.

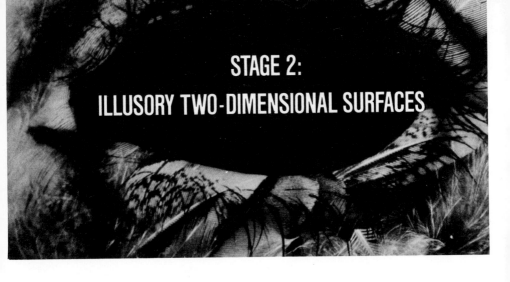

STAGE 2:
ILLUSORY TWO-DIMENSIONAL SURFACES

CONCEPT

The flatness of a two-dimensional surface invites disruption; it cannot be left alone. Many two-dimensional surfaces find themselves in the hands of those who look past surfaces as if they never existed. Employing a lengthy list of techniques including perspective, atmosphere, size differences, modelling of forms, light and shadow, the advancing and receding of colors, spatial location on the plane, and horizon lines, these masters of illusion dispel the rich emptiness of the two-dimensional surface and replace it with their own sense of space.

During the Renaissance and Baroque periods, artists were called upon to create frescoes on the walls and ceilings of the great churches of Europe, which frame heaven with their arches. Painted as illusory two-dimensional surfaces, the walls and ceiling yielded to dynamic visions of clouds and light, angels and saints, occasionally God himself. Illusory surfaces are common today, but at their first use they must have been astonishing. Just imagine the worshippers as they cast their eyes toward roof and beam only to have their gaze met by the Heavenly Host. We can catch an inkling of the magic the first Flemish and Italian painters must have worked on their contemporaries by viewing a hologram, which is a three-dimensional picture projected by laser beams. Raised to the level of art, holography could be our period's window into space.

CONTEXT

Illusions are the stuff of dreams, the magic from which magicians are made. When Narcissus first looked at his image in the mirrored surface of a pool, such a lifelike illusion was evoked that he fell in love with it. Reflecting upon that moment, let us examine briefly the motives of those who would disturb the placid plane of a two-dimensional surface with a vision of reality.

In illusory works, there is a constant questioning of what is inside, what outside. What is it that appears to lie within the boundaries of the work, and where does it become different from the world outside, which is the source of that reflection? For what possible reasons does a painter, a photographer, a film-maker, a printmaker, an architect, a product designer, a graphic artist labor to create a deep sense of space where none really existed? In a few cases the answer comes quickly. The product designer wishes to see what an object would look like if it were executed in three-dimensions. By his rendering you and I are able to react to form, color, texture, proportion, and material without having the product in front of us, just the way we select a purchase from a Sears catalog or a newspaper ad.

The factual, documentary quality of a photograph is an illusion too. We expect to see a "lifelike" representation of reality in the photo. What we really see is a very selective representation of reality as the photographer sees it. He might wish to evoke a a sense of the claustrophobia and dirt of an urban ghetto, and he does this by subtly creating his photo from an enhanced or exaggerated point-of-view.

In the fine arts, the reasons for creating illusory space are emotional and aesthetic. The only boundaries in the painter's and printmaker's world are the ones posed by the edge of the work. Here is everyspace, from the flat recession of planes in a Persian painting, to the Cubist "reliefs" of Braque, to the surrealist rooms of Magritte. Here lies the work of Escher, whose simple drawings defy perspective and the senses. Here too rests the anguished humans and animals of Beckett, trapped in their elusive boxes, frozen in silent screams within the painted surface.

Most elusive of all illusory surfaces is the filmmaker's. His colors are created by light not pigment; his perspective lies in his lenses and optical systems; his varnishes and resins are the chemistry of the processing laboratory. A painting rests on a museum wall where we may journey through its secret passages at our leisure. But a film is an experiential mode of communication. One image after another flees before our eyes. In their relationship lies their meaning. Like the build-up of texture on a surface, each unit adds its force to the next, synergistically evolving the whole picture. Each fleeting image is a function of time, and within the narrow rectangle of his frame the filmmaker has both time and space at his service. Whatever his mode, the creator of illusory two-dimensional surfaces cannot escape the mystery of his act, by which he creates truth out of deception.

APPROACHES AND MATERIALS

Using the following techniques, create a sense of depth on a two-dimensional surface. Before you start it will be helpful to have some or all of these materials handy—paper, photographs, color packs, colored pencils, crayons, acrylic paints, various density pencils for modeling with light and shade, pen and ink for line studies, perspective charts, and tracing paper.

Manipulate *dots*, now close, now far away, to suggest the modelling of surfaces by their proximity. Just as a topographical map indicates steep inclines and other surface variations, employ *line* to create a rich in-and-out movement of the surface. Using the concept of *figure and background*, create forms which float in space; enhance them through the use of *shading*. Perspective charts will assist you in seeing how *one, two, and three point perspective* can be used to build a visual space; these modes of seeing objects can be used separately or in combination. Design a space and then design objects in that space. As in film and painting, use the *atmospheric haze*, the slight softening of focus and color, to create a marked sense of depth. *Colors* advance and recede when combined in carefully studied proportion; study the work of Josef Albers and other Optical artists who have explored many possibilities in this direction. Take an object and move it about in a rectangle, toward the foreground, toward the background; study how its *change of location* creates a varying sense of space and scale of the object.

CAPTION NOTES

At an early stage in Western art, strong attempts were made by the artist to create an illusion of space on a completely flat two-dimensional surface. Early Christian and medieval art wrestled with perspective, but it wasn't until the early 14th century and the Renaissance that artists solved the problems of making two-dimensional painting appear to have spacial characteristics. Today, of course, illusory representation is a vein that has been mined almost to extinction.

The tremendous spatial range and the subtle nuances of spatial representation on a flat plane can best be seen by comparing this stage of the continuum with the one that precedes it, in which the flatness of the two-dimensional surface is maintained, and the one that follows it, in which physical texture is introduced. This second stage presents a problem as well as an opportunity in studying aesthetics because it is possible with painting to represent sculpture and architecture on illusory two-dimensional surfaces. We have the possibility of rendering the illusion of infinite space through aerial perspective; we have the option of representing plastic relief surfaces to control light sources; we can project part of the image off the picture plane through the use of color vibration; and we might even create, in the surrealist manner, strange penetrated forms that look like sculpture eroded by the wind, hanging in space. In a sense, this stage alone encompasses the whole two- and three-dimensional continuum.

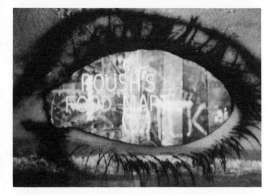

B & W A-9a, A-9b

A multiple exposure of shop windows provides an excellent transition from flat to illusory two-dimensional surfaces; we still see a respect for the flatness of the surface while the reflected images and the neon signs begin to move the eye off the surface of the picture plane. It's just as simple as that. All we're talking about at this second stage is the remarkable ability we have, through art and photography, to play tricks on the eye and to articulate a two-dimensional surface, through various techniques, so that it reads as though it were a three-dimensional surface.

The surround of the Eye has been changed to a seascape for this stage of the continuum. Its photographic illusion of great distance toward a horizon makes an interesting contrast with the artistic illusions presented within the Eye in our seven Stage 2 images.

B&W A-10a, A-10b

In this woodcut, we see the beginnings of some marvelous tricks that the artist can play with the human visual system. We see that tantalizingly real fish seem to be lying on a flat plane created by radiating lines analogous to those used in the optical painting we studied in Stage 1 (A-6). The curved lines which describe the fish forms, by delineating the scales on the surface of their bodies, run directly opposite to the lines of the background, and it is this which emphasizes the quality of relief.

Woodcuts, which place great premium on the use of line to describe form, create shallow spatial illusions at best. The visual space of this relief is probably no more than three-quarters of an inch off the picture plane. Yet it is clearly representational of a third dimension. When we can articulate form so it moves off the surface like this, we obviously have set out on the road of illusory representation.

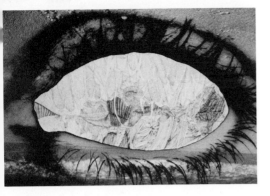

B&W A-11a, A-11b

Value, or contrast in terms of light and dark, enters our lexicon of spatial illusory devices in this India-ink drawing on a yellow ground. Value immediately gives a sense of projection from the flat surface of the picture plane. The darker the color value of an area, the more it tends to recede into the surface, almost as if burrowing little holes into the interior of the illusory projection. Lighter values, such as those in the leaves and tendrils, tend to rise off the picture plane. The middle values, represented by parallel contour lines in the upper third of the drawing, give only a slight illusion of movement toward us. The visual space of this relief is probably about five to six inches forward, a higher illusion than the fish woodcut (A-10). Inward, a much deeper space is represented by the dark objects in the center line.

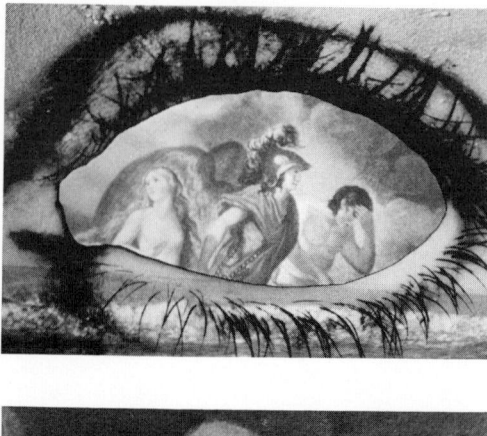

B&W A-12 a, A-12b

This 18th-century illustration from Milton's *Paradise Lost* shows us that color is an important additional dimension to projections in space. It is generally true that warm colors, such as the reds in the angel's garments, advance, and that cool colors, such as the dominant blue tonality of this painting, recede. Our subjective experience of the nearness of warm earth tones and the inaccessibility of the cool blue sky is, surprisingly, repeated in our own physiology. The cones in the human visual membrane are on the inside of the retina, and transmit warm colors to the brain, while the rods are farther back in that literal physiological space, and transmit the cool end of the spectrum. We should be wary, however, of the old wive's tale that warms *always* advance and cools *always* recede. Modern color theory suggests that projections are more closely related to the massing of the color, the degree to which it is used in terms of total area.

When dealing with traditional illusions of space, such as this almost tactile representation of figures modelled by light and shade, we rarely find attempts to project forward from the picture plane. It always seems to be a picture window into space, as if we were looking into nature. Here the cloud forms descend through successive planes deep into the interior, and both the photographic seascape of the surround and the painting project back from the foreground defined by the Eye. The eyelashes, however, seem to move toward us.

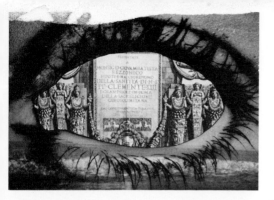

One would be hard pressed to determine whether this 18th-century Piranesi engraving is a photograph of a monument, or an artist's representation, so real is the illusion. Italy is the Renaissance nation most preoccupied with this kind of illusion, and the engraving follows the stylistic canons employed in creating photographic impressions of relief surfaces. In essence the technique is to create the illusion of a consistent light source as similar to physical reality as possible. During daylight hours, the sun mainly comes from the south in Italy and other northern hemisphere nations, therefore the artistic creation of a light source emulates nature in that it seems to come from the upper right in order to be consistent with our expectations of reality.

Perhaps the most unique aspect of 20th century painting has been this preoccupation with spatial illusion. Both Juan Gris and Georges Braque were masters at popping the object off the picture plane, keeping the integrity of the surface, and punching forms into the picture plane.

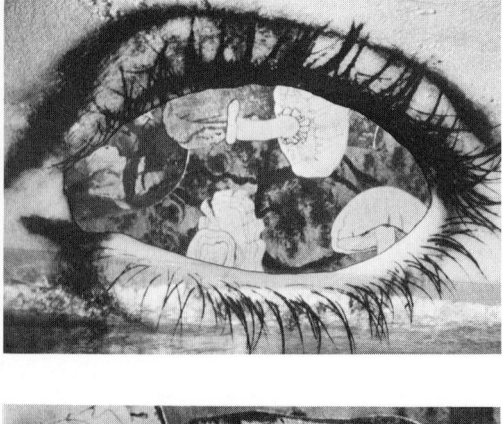

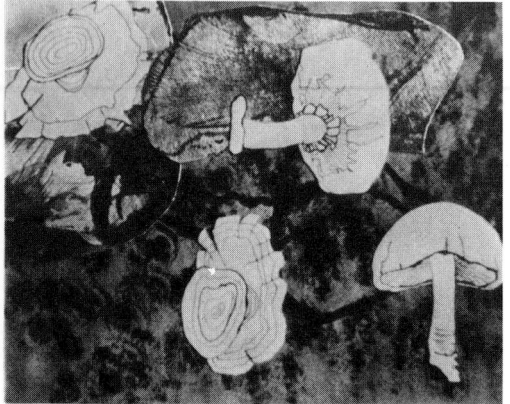

B&W A-14a, A-14b,

Line, shape, perspective, atmosphere, and color, all of the tools that have been forged through the centuries to create spatial illusion, are put to use in this student project. The mushroom shapes are floating around off the picture plane; the middle ground works as a halfway point that represents the surface plane of the painting; the areas of murky plant forms seem to dig into the space, falling back from the surface plane. All in all there is a visual space of about several feet here, an interesting comparison to the vast aerial perspectives in the *Paradise Lost* illustration (A-12) or the high relief dimensions shown in the Piranesi engraving (A-13).

B&W A-15a, A-15b, A-15c

Part of our problem in the 20th century is a terrible visual boredom. Virtually everything has been tried so many times that we're jaded to normal illusory effects, and we crave more and more bizarre and obtuse visual images. And so we end this section on spatial illusion with a very dramatic photographic montage created from a shot of White Sands National Monument at six o'clock in the morning with a shot of a road surface oil slick which we then projected into this moon-like shape.

Sometimes photographic reality can look more like art than art, and we have chosen this bit of artistic license to end Stage 2 of the continuum because it clearly says that we can do anything with space, and you know it, and we know it. That's what we're up to, that's what's happening here.

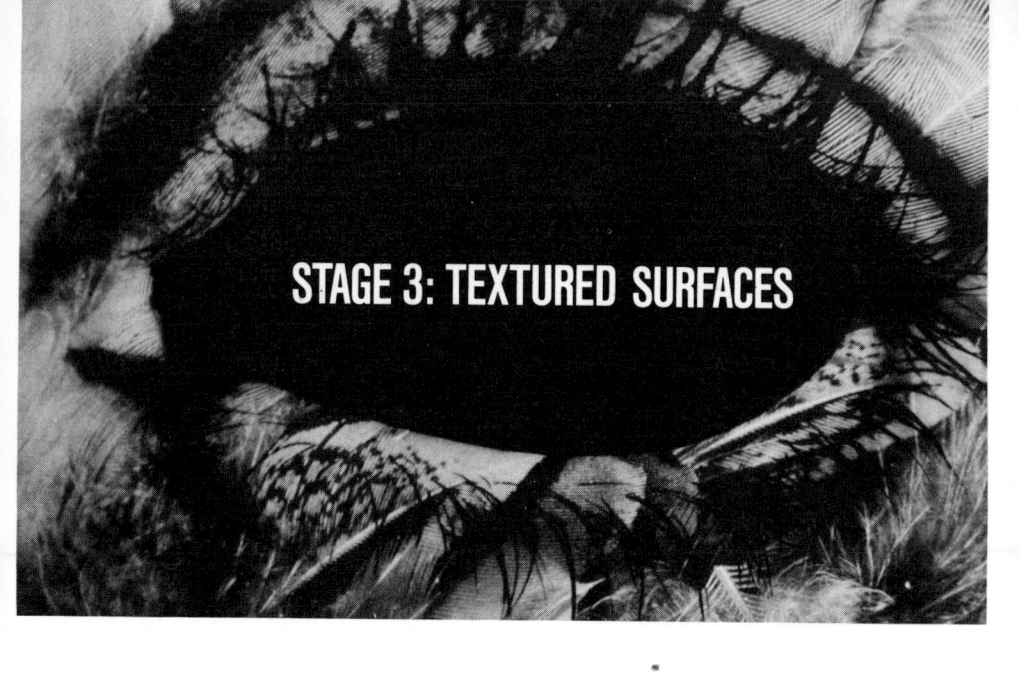

STAGE 3: TEXTURED SURFACES

CONCEPT

With the flat surface ruptured by illusion, it is but one more step to introduce actual texture on that surface. All surfaces have a textural feeling to them. We respond visually to the roughness of handhewn lumber, the softness of cat's fur, the polish of Plexiglas, and the patina of pewter as if we were actually touching them.

Light, shade, and modelling play a major role in our ability to perceive texture. A perfectly flat surface that is evenly illuminated does not appear to have any bumps, projections, or modulations. But with a textured surface, one is drawn immediately to the often tiny projections as they catch the light, forming areas of highlight and shadow. These small bumps pushing upward from the flat plane are the basic units from which texture is created and recognized.

In texture, the effect of the whole takes precedence over the parts of which it is comprised. Repeated over and over, varying slightly in scale, the units merge into whole areas of texture. Once we are able to identify any single textural unit clearly, its emergence as a separate projection on the plane signals another category in the continuum, that of low relief. In terms of the design continuum, textured surfaces are the first upward movement into space of the original flat plane. Conversely, we can see in the miniature hills and valleys of the surface the first real intrusions of space into the interface which separates the worlds of two and three dimensions.

CONTEXT

Selecting a hat? Throwing a pot? Mixing a salad? The quality of texture plays a role in most of our day-to-day choices and in how we feel about what we touch and see. We talk about texture in music, although we cannot touch it, because music comes so close to us through our sense of hearing. We feel it wrapping around us like the clothes we wear. In the same way, visual texture constantly touches us through our sense of sight, while mowing a lawn, polishing our shoes, or furnishing our homes. Textured surfaces help us get a better grip on things, both physically and visually.

Designers consciously use the quality of textured surfaces in their products and artists manipulate texture in their works because of the strong, often unconscious response we all have to it. It can make us want to reach out and bring the object close to us or prevent us from ever seeing past the surface.

Nature is an immense warehouse of surfaces, from shiny moist mushrooms to the plush cushions of ferns and mosses. Tree bark and rock, leaves and fields of grass, forested hillsides, and the rippled waters of a small lake all are a feast for the searching eye. Similarly, the city's streets with their shiny chrome cars, burgeoning reflecting windows, roughened pavement, weathered brick and wood, and the faces of young and old alike form endless compositions of textures.

APPROACHES AND MATERIALS

Discover how nature evolves its compositions by studying a variety of natural surfaces. Photograph them. Draw them. Collect them. Then create a piece of nature; try to fit the parts, the individual surfaces, together so that they look like they have never been separate. Your materials might be found objects, ground clay mixed with rubber cement, sand, pebbles, papier mâché, natural grainy materials like small beans. Stack them, glue them, spray them with paint.

Create a textural painting. Use the natural colors of the objects. Use paint.

Find textural units in a store: cereals, cookies, peas, grain, birdseed, glass, sandpaper, woodchips, candies, foil, cloth, burlap, gauze, nails, drinking straws. Create compositions with only one kind of unit, then with several kinds. Paint over the texture. Make all the units white. All black. Paint texture directly on the surface by mixing it first with the paints.

Try to create surfaces in which the texture seems to be a natural part of the surface rather than something applied later.

CAPTION NOTES

Textured surfaces are the beginning of the emergence of three-dimensional reality from the two-dimensional plane, a netherland between the illusory forms of Stage 2 and the full reliefs of Stage 4. Texture, as distinct from relief, is the slight upward projection of many portions of the surface, in a scale that is so small in relation to the surface that we do not perceive the convexities and concavities as independent units but as overall modulation of the plane.

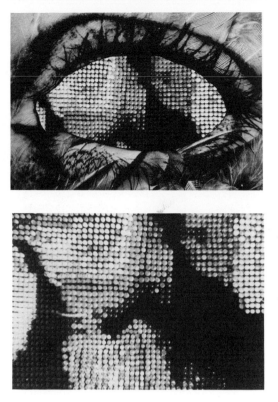

B&W A-16 a, A-16b

In this project, which demonstrates both illusory and physical projection from the two-dimensional plane, the scale of the texture is the same in all parts. The modules are paint-filled gelatin capsules, arranged so that the colors produce an illusionary visual space similar to the effect in A-12. The warm colors seem to come forward from a surface defined by the matte black area. This is the first example in which there is both illusory and physical projection off the picture plane into space.

For this stage of the continuum, the surround of the eye is a photograph of beautiful soft feathers, which are excellent for textured surface projects as well as for collages. Another excellent texturing material, vermiculite, is available at any nursery or floral shop. Powdered in a blender and mixed with rubber cement or Elmer's glue, it forms stable relief surfaces.

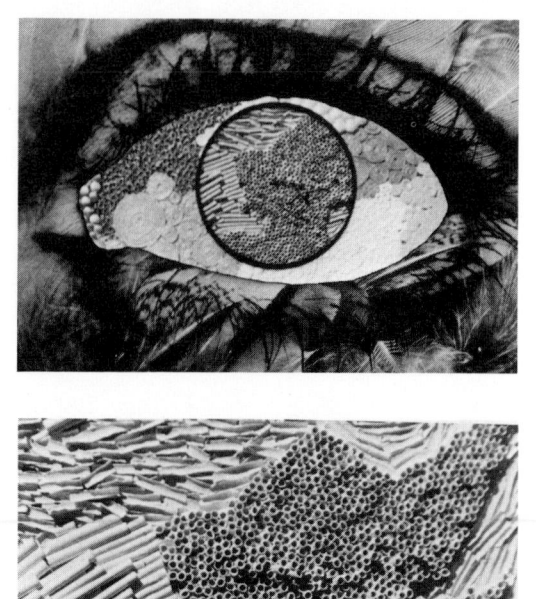

B&W A-17a, A-17b, A-17c

Two textured, monochromatic compositions by students introduce the concept of variations of scale in a relief surface. In the center of the Eye, repeated units in the same scale help emphasize nuances of texture, while units of different size in the surrounding collage emphasize the scale of the relief. Black-and-white illustrations A-17b and A-17c show these compositions in full. The central collage is composed of cut soda straws standing face up or used as contrasting linear elements. The surrounding collage is created from painted string, cereal, and cookies.

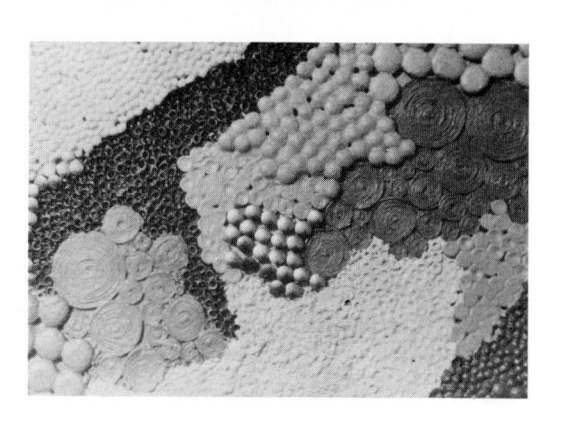

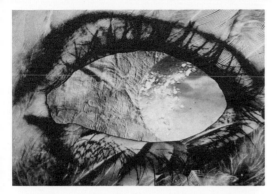

B&W A-18a, A-18b, A-18c

A similar range of warm, rich tonality in two very different subjects presents an interesting juxtaposition of textured surfaces. The student composition on the left is composed of painted cloth and net, producing a very earth-like feeling. This is sensitively reflected in a photograph of colored muds from the "paint pots" in Yellowstone National Park and in the feather arrangement projected in the surround of the Eye.

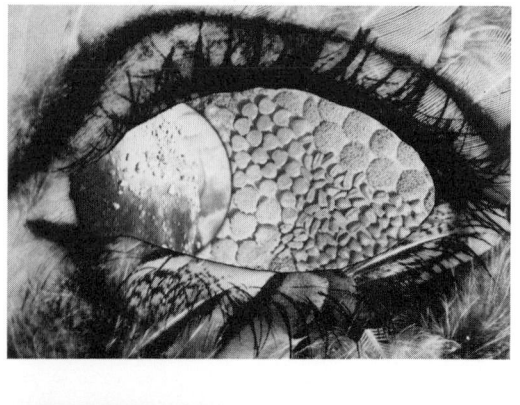

B&W A-19a, A-19b, A-19c

Here, another earth study from Yellowstone Park is contrasted with a student collage worked from such ephemeral materials as cookies, candy, and nuts, all painted in warm earth tones. The round shapes of both studies help to contrast the different textural effects that can be obtained by varying the scale of the relief units. The black-and-white illustration of the student composition shows how careful the artist was to change not only the texture of various objects but also the relative sizes.

It's not a bad idea to have a sense of humor when you are involved in the study of design; we should not always think of the work of Art with a capital A. The warm sense of humor implied by using cookies and candy in art helps students guard against the inevitable lofty postures they assume in relationship to their own talent, perhaps to defend themselves against the impact of the full weight of the history of art, and on top of that, the enormous challenge of the talents of their instructors and peers.

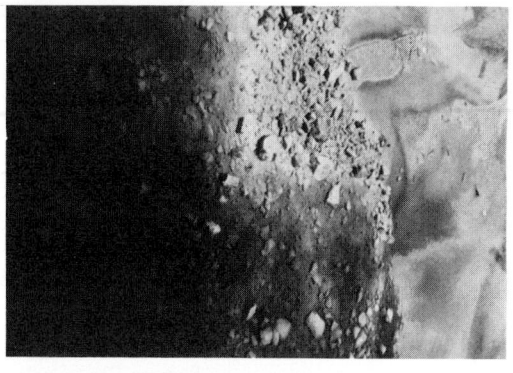

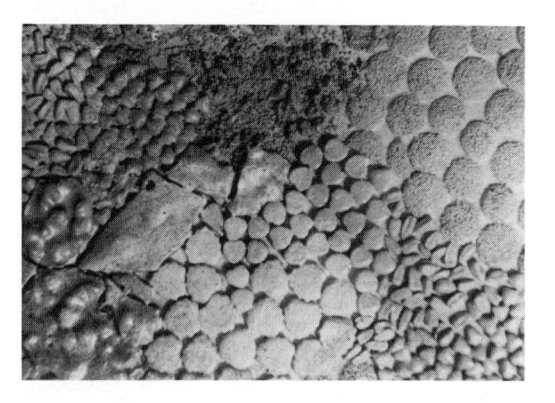

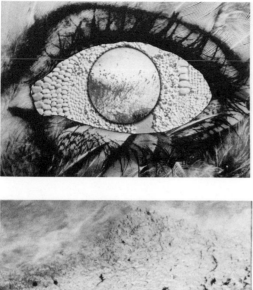

B&W A-20a, A-20b, A-20c

Shape as well as scale has been varied in the contrasting studies here, while the element of color is so muted that the texture reads almost entirely in terms of value contrasts. The Piranesi engraving we presented in the last stage of the continuum (A-13) used an illusory light source to achieve relief effects in a monochromatic color scheme similar to this one. In illusory surfaces, changes in color strongly suggest visual movement forward, back, off, into, and away from the picture plane. In the same way, when dealing with real three-dimensional surfaces, the actual color of the object used has a great deal of significance in the way it reads texturally, as can be seen by a comparison of this slide with A-18 and A-19. When using aerosol paint, try not to destroy the possible effects of texture due to natural colors which are eliminated in the simple unity of the overall coat of a single paint color.

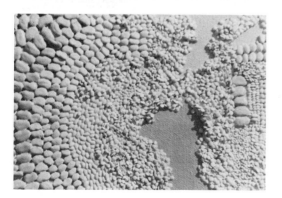

B&W A-21a, A-21b, A-21c

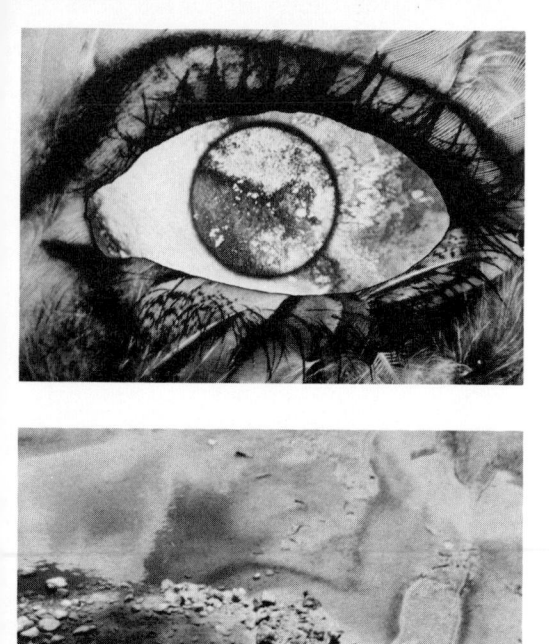

This last comparison of two earth studies from Yellowstone National Park shows how closely art and nature can come in their texture effects. The surrounding photograph is of lichen crusted granite. Some of the most elegant textured surfaces can be found in granite cliffs, where the various rock faces and forms have been twisted and reconstituted through the enormous forces of the earth-building process that created the granite. We are asking our students to move out into nature and look closely at the infinite variety of textured surfaces there—earth, leaves, feathers, skin, fish eyes, sandpaper, hemp. One could spend a lifetime exploring the visual possibilities of just this one stage of the design continuum.

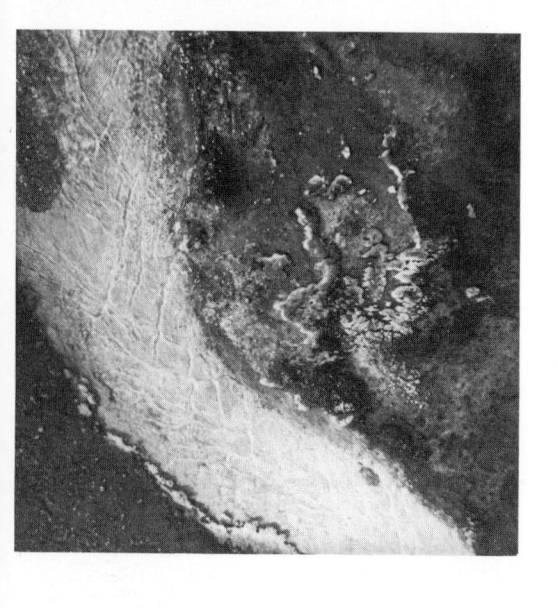

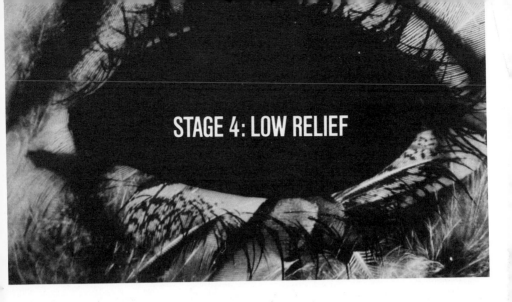

STAGE 4: LOW RELIEF

CONCEPT

The progression upward from a flat plane continues. What were small bumps are now definite lines or shapes. What was surface embellishment is now the movement of the very surface itself.

Low relief is marked by the increased role of light and shadow in revealing form. Light falls on the now more individualized projections from the ground plane and casts shadows in the recessions. As an interface between the forces of mass and space, the relief surface begins a restrained movement outward, as if the potential energy lying beneath the surface of the relief is still too weak to resist the great pressure of space. But it is at the interface, in those subtle incursions into the surface, that the hints of future happenings begin to reveal themselves in the shallow signs of things to come.

CONTEXT

The bas reliefs of the ancient Egyptians, those cryptic incisions in stone, are among the greatest examples of low relief. Print-making techniques that involve intaglio surfaces, where the engraving plate is chiseled with tools or acid, produce prints with raised surfaces. Even without ink we can see the design as the light plays on the surface of the paper.

But one need not turn to art history for examples from this stage of the design continuum. Low reliefs are all about us, in the weathered walls of our buildings, the surfaces of our stones and stoves, the veins of leaves, the craftsman's subtle imprint on a bowl or serving tray, the stamped edges on a license plate, the cracks in the sidewalk, or the monogram on a handkerchief or sheet of personal stationery.

Think of how many objects we use everyday which are embossed, incised, stamped, chased, or ridged. Though the fine edges which catch the light and the narrow channels which hold the shadows often make these items hard to clean, we willingly accept the difficulty because the decorations create a sense of light and life in otherwise undistinguished surfaces, subtly breaking up the plainness of the plane.

APPROACHES AND MATERIALS

Take a large leaf. Make a wax impression of it using paraffin. Try this with other objects. Combine one set of imprints with another of differing character. Scribe the wax with a hot tool.

Cast a plaster surface in a mold made from a concave object. Using chisels, nails, knives, and other sharp tools, scratch and gouge that surface. Try to create shapes, rhythms and patterns.

Take string, buttons, washers, and other small found objects and generate a surface using them. Cover the surface with glue or wax and paint it.

Starting with foil, press various objects into the metal, retaining their impression. Create a composition out of your discoveries.

Talk to a printmaker about woodblocks, etching and engraving, and collography. Study their techniques and apply them to a wood or linoleum block. You will need sharp cutting tools, ink or paint, sturdy paper, and a spoon for burnishing.

CAPTION NOTES

In low relief, projections and recessions on the surface begin to dominate the over-all modulation of the surface texture, although the integrity of the surface is still maintained. Low relief is a hybrid—it clings closely to the surface plane but hints at the emerging truth of three-dimensional mass. In trying to define this stage of the continuum, we must talk about form as a function of scale in inches, feet, miles, or even light years. Huge galaxies in outer space when reinterpreted by computer analysis of radio photographs may be only six inches wide on the surface of a newspaper page, while in reality light takes eleven million years to reach from one end of the object to the other. The absolute size of the image cannot be used to interpret the scale of the relief; rather it is how far away the surface seems to be from the viewer's eye.

Light plays a great part in creating this visual distance scale; the light patterns on the form determine its peaks and valleys. The deeper the drop in space the darker the shadow; the more the plane of the sculpture is inclined toward the light source, the lighter the value and the brighter the highlight. In a way, this stage turns the previous ones around. We are now using form to paint light and dark.

B&W A-22a, A-22b

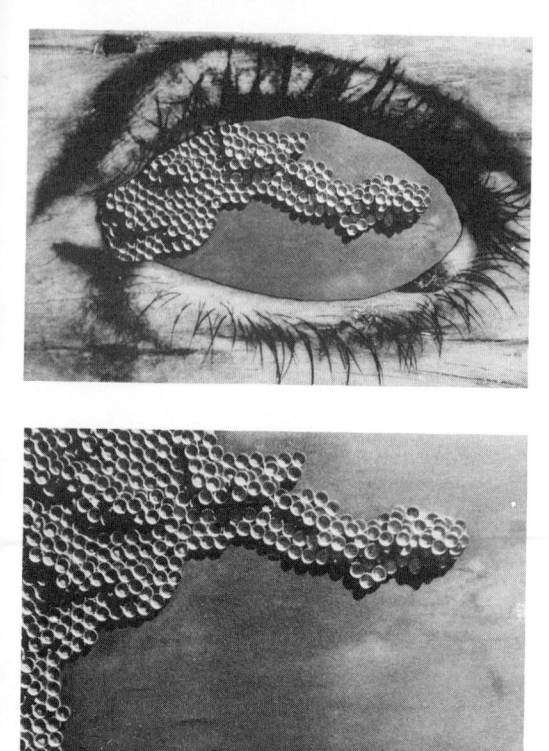

This handsomely painted project is constructed from bottle caps on Masonite, yet if I were to let my imagination wander, I would say that I am looking down on a wind-eroded range from an altitude of perhaps 100 miles up. This effect is achieved, as in the illusory Piranesi engraving in A-13, by the traditional Western European convention of light falling on the object from the upper right and shadowing on the lower left. A relief cannot be constructed by placing an object here and there without also looking at it in many different light sources as it is evolving. A beautiful pattern in one light angle may look very disappointing when the lighting changes. In studying the black-and-white illustration of this project it is interesting to postulate how the object would look if it were illuminated from the bottom instead of the top.

The Eye surround is now a weathered log which creates a flat but textured plane from which the reliefs rise or descend in our six images in this stage of the continuum. The eyelashes create an interesting scale comparison, sometimes seeming to project out over a great distance on the surround, while the slight projections and indentations in the surface of the wood illustrate the basic concept of low relief.

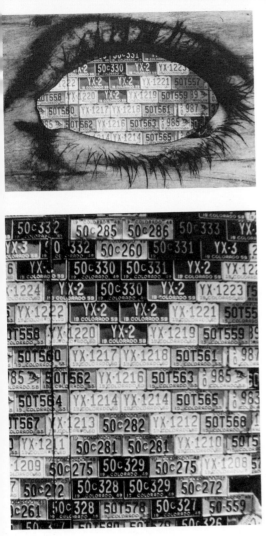

B&W A-23a, A-23b

We're just having some fun here with a photograph of a side of a garage in Colorado that is covered with license plates. The stamped, slightly raised edges and numerals create subtle highlights and shadows across the entire surface that beautifully illustrate the concept of low relief. The more one studies this architectural wall, the more one finds in it. Sometimes life is greater than art! Strong use of light and dark plates creates big geometric patterns such as the bold X in light plates that can be seen fully in the black-and-white illustration. There is a progression in numbers, from 1209 on the lower left, which increases toward the upper right, adding a rather whimsical arithmetic element to this low relief. One can't help but wonder where the artist was able to collect these sequential license plates. Perhaps he worked in a prison and managed to sequester them. Whatever he did, he has combined the tactile sentiments of the sculptor, who is always involved with physical entities, with the more abstract, cerebral images of the painter, who is always held to the two-dimensional plane.

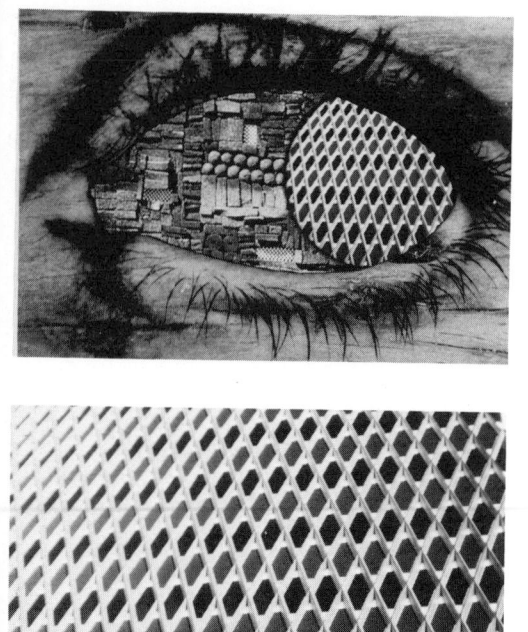

B&W A-24a, A-24b, A-24c

With this comparison of a student project in foam blocks and carved forms and a detail of the facade of a Pittsburgh skyscraper (on the right) we begin a serious study of low relief scale. Obviously the building is much larger in dimension than the student work. Yet the two appear to be in aesthetic sympathy because of the distances from which the pieces were photographed, the building from several hundred yards and the construction from only a few feet. The changing shapes and degree of relief in the student project contrast with the uniform latticework relief of the building facade. Neither one, however, violates the premise of low relief, in which the surface plane must dominate the texture of the projections and recessions from it, no matter how high they are in actual measurements. This is what distinguishes low relief from high relief.

Two parts of a railroad train present an interesting contrast in the effects of color and materials on just slightly modulated relief surfaces. The projections from the rich metallic surface of the steam engine and the penetrations into the wood plane of the box car are no higher than some of the examples of our textured surfaces, yet they are not overall modulations of the plane but independent units. This is what distinguishes low relief from textured surfaces. We are also playing here with the difference between an illusory visual depth created by the strong graphic value contrasts in the red, white, and black logo of the boxcar and the subtler, but actual, relief created by the texture of its wood, nails, and board edges, all defined by a light source falling from the upper right. Introducing the elements of the painter's craft in relief forms or sculpture produces very complex visual experiences. Shadow, rather than color, creates the strongest relief effect on the boiler, with the rivet heads popping up into space from the thick steel plates of the boiler. With flat lighting, you would hardly be able to read this picture at all. When we move from illusory surfaces into three dimensional surfaces, the artist's concern for and use of light is very much part of his total aesthetic.

B&W A-26a, A-26b, A-26c

In a way, low relief is still very much a painterly activity, and one has to think long and hard about value contrasts and the importance of light in defining the relief. Our two objects here differ in the use of value and color as well as in total dimensions, but relate well because of the way light falls on shallow reliefs of the same scale. On the left, a student project in carved wax creates a relief by incising projections that rise from the surface. Only on the upper right, which can be seen in the black-and-white illustration, does the penetration go down behind the general plane of the relief, all of which has been painted in the same tone, thus emphasizing the value contrasts quite sharply. The detail on the right is from one of the Watts Towers in Los Angeles, uncommissioned monumental structures created by a mad genius who was free to explore bizarre avenues of expression. This relief is built upwards from the surface by a rich incrustation of found objects, mosaic patterns, reverse scales and a shallow texture of imprints of objects. Both reliefs shown in the Eye are created by projections rising from the surface, but the projections themselves are textured in opposite ways. The wax is carved into, while the concrete is added to in a mosaic treatment that allows the sculptor to introduce color into relief in a very effective way.

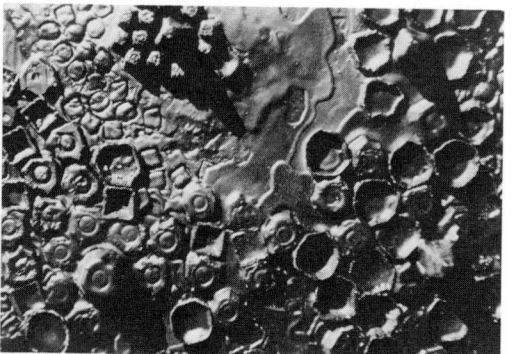

B&W A-27a, A-27b, A-27c

Here, in the contrast between two monochromatic reliefs, we can see the important part played by the form of the projections. Although the piece at the left is a paper sculpture, created from cut and incised bristol board forced into relief form and then assembled in a cluster of modular units, and the detail on the right is a stone relief on a church in Oaxaca, Mexico, there is in both a feeling of growing things, of plant and leaf forms that have entwined themselves in a sensuous surface. We must not forget that low relief has a tactile physical being as well as being molded visually from light and dark. One could experience a relief in a completely dark room by feeling the surface with one's fingers, something that cannot be done with a painting. To return to our organic analogy, a modular relief is like a plant, which repeats its leaf form over and over again, sometimes small, sometimes large. Perhaps there is a lesson to be learned here, that in any creation it is good to limit the range of forms to arrive at a strong aesthetic statement.

49

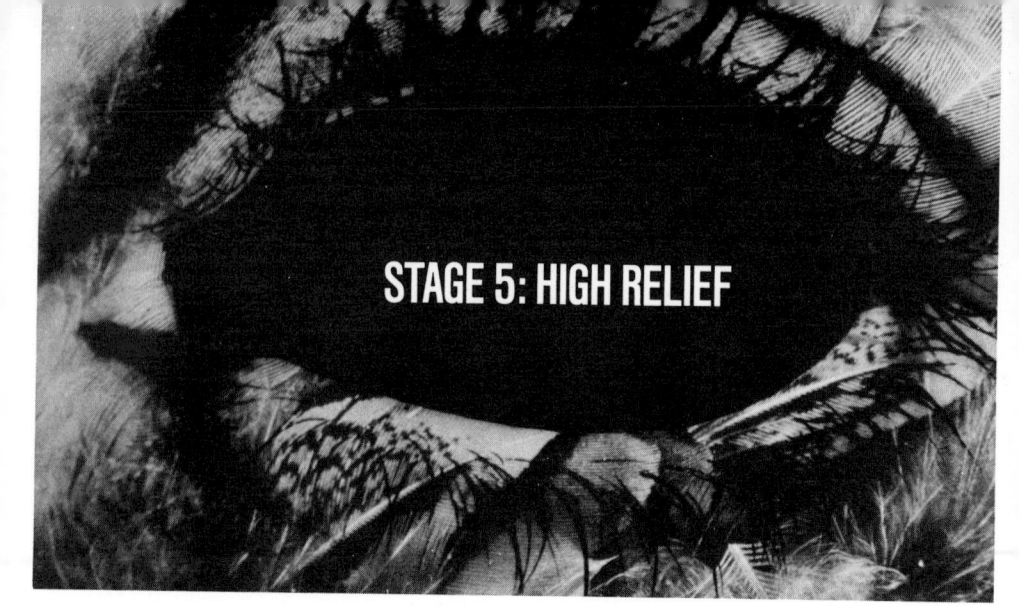

STAGE 5: HIGH RELIEF

CONCEPT

High relief is an explosive equilibrium between mass and space. Projections are super-projections, recessions are almost cave-like. It is at this stage in the continuum that we first realize the strong forces at work in the mass-space relationship. Pressing ever harder into and out of the surface, these are forces that would break the interface if it did not bend with them. But all the while, we are not free of the ground plane; high relief is still a surface, with aspects of the world in two dimensions. It is still essentially frontal, that is, perceived like other two-dimensional objects from one view only, the view of an observer located directly in front of it.

Its strong modelling and pronounced forms are revealed to us in an exaggerated contrast between light and shadow. High reliefs are clearly forms in transition, in progress between two worlds, not quite two-dimensional surfaces any longer, not yet three-dimensional objects.

CONTEXT

The forces of nature, particularly erosion by wind and water, provide us with many spectacular examples of high relief. One can almost feel the abstract concept of space cutting into mass in the analogy with wind and water as they cut grotesque sandstone pillars and giant mesas, incredible canyons and precarious cliffs.

So too, an aerial view of most towns and cities creates a sense of high relief, as if the buildings were nearly piled on top of one another. And higher than that, certain dense cloud formations create very strong relief forms when viewed from above, as the sun casts deep shadows into the soft valleys of mist.

A child ruffles a blanket and creates mountains and valleys; junk yards and garbage heaps provide more, if less pleasant, examples; cereal boxes, soup cans, meat and fruit stacked row on row in the supermarket all suggest high relief surfaces.

APPROACHES AND MATERIALS

Glue found objects—wheels, pulleys, gears, blocks—to a surface in a dense arrangement. Spray-paint them one color to create a unified sense of surface, where all objects work together, and none stand out.

Nail objects to a board. Make a plaster mold from the new surface. Cast into the mold. Compare the negative and positive reliefs of the same surface.

Make a plaster cast using cups or bowls as molds, just as you used your pail when you were a child making castles in the sand. Arrange your castles on a surface, some high, some low, creating a new relief out of them. In the same way, arrange throwaway coffee cups of different heights and diameters to create an architectural relief on a table top. Paint it to enhance the effect of light and shadow on the forms.

CAPTION NOTES

We introduce this stage of the continuum with a comparison of three images, one from each relief stage Image A-22 is a small student work in low relief; image A-28 is a high relief photographed from the air in Bryce Canyon, Utah; image A-34 is an environmental relief shown in a photograph of Monument Valley, Utah.

The comparison makes it clear what we mean by the term design continuum. Although the three stages of relief are obviously divided arbitrarily by the authors, they show successive movement up into space from a flat plane. Low relief is the closest to painting, although it shares with high relief the subordination of the individual forms to the total visual effect, as can be seen in the bottle cap construction (with a scale in inches) and the rocks from Bryce Canyon (with a scale in yards). Environmental relief is the closest to architecture in the prominence of its individual forms, although it shares with high relief the dependence of sculptural forms on a surface plane, as can be seen when the crowded, eroded forms of Bryce Canyon are compared to the dominant buttes of Monument Valley (with a scale in miles).

In defining the differences between these stages, we must recognize that our division depends on the relation of physical size to the vantage point of the observer. Another way of putting it is that the ratio between the plane of the relief and the projections forward in space is different at each of these stages. We do not want to draw a direct numerical ratio, but hope that the relative size of plane and projection will become visually obvious as we go first through the six images in high relief and then the seven images in environmental relief. We can legitimately compare a student work that is little more than a foot in diameter with the facade of a church that is about 100 feet high because the projections, an inch or so in one case and six feet in the other, fall roughly in the same scale. It is important to realize that we have placed our three introductory images in different stages not because of the size of the pictured landscape but because of the relation between the size of the projections and the size of the plane.

A-22　　　　　　　　A-28　　　　　　　　A-34

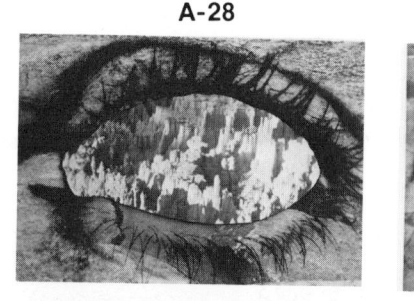

B&W A-28a, A-28b

In the black-and-white illustration of the eroded rock forms in Bryce Canyon, one can easily see that high relief is essentially a single plane articulated in such a manner that we are always aware that the forms are resting on the same flat, base. The contours tell us that this is a series of thin wafers of rock that have been eaten away by wind and water but once were all part of the same slice through the plane. The emergence of such sculptured form from two-dimensional surfaces tells the visual story about the emergence of high relief in our continuum.

The Eye surround for this stage is a close photograph of a pitted and cracked rock face, with deep shadows in the cracks producing the high-relief effect. It is interesting to compare the scale of the eyelashes here, where they seem like frail plants growing on the rock face, to the giant projections they seemed to be on the less deformed wooden surface of the surround in our fourth stage of low relief.

What is the difference between the high relief represented by the stone jaguar head from Jalapa, Mexico, and that of the painted student project created from actual three-dimensional found objects? We can see that the essential characteristic of high relief is penetration of three-dimensional form into space. If, in the student project, the objects were not attached to, or describing, a surface, they would be full sculptural forms, not parts of a relief. As it is, the student work is only modestly successful, because the arrangement of the forms is somewhat haphazard, and given only superficial unity by an overall coat of paint. The stone head, however, is a superb example of high relief, where the sculptor has succeeded in literally drawing with light. Notice how the shadow under the eyelid is the result of a deep undercutting of the stone, and how the pitted surface adds to the total textural effect.

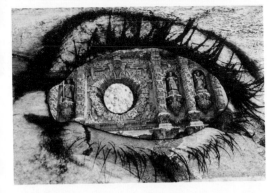

B&W A-30a, A-30b, A-30c

A student project of painted card-board, dowels, straw, and wood is superimposed on the window of a richly embellished church facade in Taxco, Mexico. Scale comparison becomes important here, and we can best study it by comparing the black-and-white illustrations of the two subjects. The shadows of sun-light falling on some of the straws in the construction give us a hint that the forms rise off the plane quite a bit, as much as a third of the foot-long diameter of the piece. This is why we have included it as high relief. The church facade, about 100 feet high, is a rich, almost Moorish example of textured surfaces and carved low-relief decorations on the architectural high-relief ele-ments—columns, pilasters, doors, windows—which project as much as six feet in some cases. This scale of relief is roughly the same as the student project, which also has a richly clustered effect of vari-ous forms and heights of relief projections.

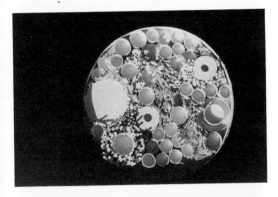

B&W A-31a, A-31b, A-31c

Our composite photograph shows two student projects of very different materials, although the scales of the reliefs are the same. Because of this similarity we have taken the liberty of surrounding the physically larger object, a relief composition of painted shoes, by the physically smaller one, a plaster relief created of relief-sculptured clay which was then cast in plaster. The methods of construction are also quite dissimilar. The shoe collage is an additive way of creating a relief. It is whimsically constructed of shoes and pieces of shoes pulled together successfully by painting so that they read as a handsome pattern of horizontals and verticals rather than as utilitarian objects. The clay form is subtractive relief. A wonderfully simple and sensuous surface invites one to find by touch the interstices and surfaces of the human form from which it seems to have been derived. The piece appears to have been created by digging into a thick slab of clay with modelling tools until this beautiful form was achieved.

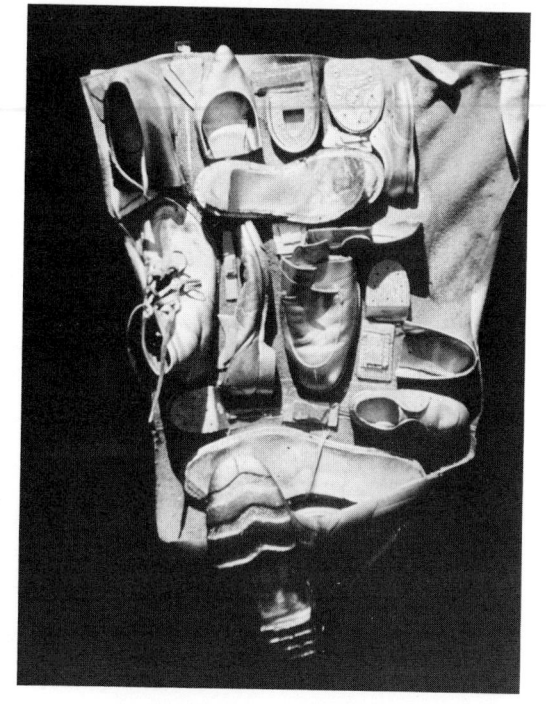

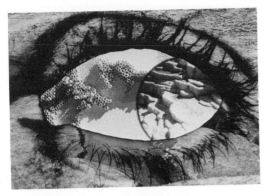

B&W A-32a, A-32b, A-32c

A rock formation from Yellowstone National Park and a student project created from clusters of cut plastic straws in a sensitive color scheme much like the rocks give us a further insight into the way light and shadow are manipulated to describe multiple planes in relief forms. We can see that both of these reliefs are created from a series of step-like surfaces, each of which reiterates the essential horizontal flat plane on which the entire relief resides. The stone steps of the natural formation look as if they had been carved by Indians making a primitive rock environment for themselves. In the straw relief, each cluster of straws defines a new level of space which restates the surface from which it rises. The level at the top of the photograph is possibly less than an inch high, and many groupings restate this lowest level of relief. But if we follow the shadows as the ensuing steps move up into space, we can see that at some point the straws must project off the surface at least three inches, high enough to make this high relief. The skill with which such shadows can be created by the precipitous nature of constructed forms is part of the stuff of which good relief artists are made.

B&W A-33a, A-33b

We have saved the best for last. This high relief of simple, strong forms, textured by an outer covering of mosaic, was created for a wall in the University of Mexico in Mexico City, where it is one of the highlights of the campus. Hundreds of feet across and about 50 or 60 feet high it combines beautiful mosaic color, which defines the form in a painterly sense, with elegant monumental forms that remind us of Giotto and Fra Angelico. The two black-and-white illustrations show us how remarkable this monumental work is at any distance.

STAGE 6: ENVIRONMENTAL RELIEF

CONCEPT

Little more can be done *to* a surface than to create configurations of high relief, as seen in the last section. But things can happen *on* the surface, particularly if we think of that surface as a landscape or an environment. Forms existing in the context of a larger environment are considered environmental reliefs. Architects at their best carefully consider the relationship between a building they are designing and the setting in which it will be placed. Will the building reflect its surroundings harmoniously? Will it contrast with neighboring architectural features or does it have the feel of belonging where it is to be built?

In terms of the design continuum, this evolution of form represents the beginning of a separate life of forms in space. Environmental relief forms, whether small or large, exist in their larger context, not yet completely free from any attachments to a surrounding, although they must be considered as completed forms in themselves rather than merely projections of the surface plane.

CONTEXT

There are numerous historical solutions to the architecture-landscape problem coming to us from varied cultures. The environment may be thought of in many different ways, not always strictly physical. The Egyptians located the pyramids with regard to astronomical features such as the rising and setting of certain stars, in what one might call an environment of the cosmos. Later, the Greeks built temples and theaters at locations for their natural beauty, each demonstrating in some way the forces of nature and the universe as manifested through the god to whom they were dedicated. Medieval fortress towns actually built their own environment around them in the form of protective walls and moats. These walled cities are unusually integrated environmental reliefs because the surroundings and architecture are constructed out of the same materials. Gardens have frequently been considered a most important part of the whole, as in the meditative setting of a Japanese house and garden or the splendor of the formal gardens at the Palace of Versailles.

Everywhere we turn we see forms in the context of surroundings, and it is the conscious or unconscious placement of these forms that determine our relationship to our world. We cannot arrange furniture or hang a picture, park a car in a huge lot, or move a chesspiece on a gameboard without expressing the principles of environmental relief.

APPROACHES AND MATERIALS

Take a found object that you have selected for its exciting or beautiful form and create a background for it that enhances the object. Now look around and criticize or praise examples of integration of architecture and landscape in your town.

Design an article of jewelry for your arm or neck. Consider the relationship between body form and jewelry form. Now design a beautiful city with trees, parks, and buildings.

Create an abstract surface of plaster, wax, cardboard, paper, Styrofoam (plastic foam), wood, or clay. Locate forms within that environment. Now study Frank Lloyd Wright and his philosophy, select a landscape in your town or from a photograph, and design a house that works with the land not against it.

CAPTION NOTES

All along in these last four stages of Part 1, we have been trying to show the relation of the scale and position of the mass to its greater environment. Yet there is no feature on the face of the earth that has any significance in terms of what the earth really is, a huge ball hanging in the vacuum of space. If we go 240,000 miles out as the astronauts have, and look back, the earth is just a blue marble. Huge natural forms and monumental architectural forms would not be even a speck from that distance. Yet from very close up small forms may have a scale that reminds us of the great contours of the earth. It is only our vantage point in relation to the mass that determines how we define it and how we describe it.

We have already discussed this photograph of natural earth forms at Monument Valley, Utah, in our introduction to high relief. These buttes go a long way to stating the obvious about environmental relief. We call such forms, which are 300 or 400 feet high, environmental relief only because they sit on a plane about 35 miles across. If we were to go close enough in viewing these masses so that their dependence on the earth's surface, from which they rise as relief, were no longer clear, then we would call them sculptural forms.

The Eye surround has been changed to an extreme close up of a lushly colored leaf. The contrast of the very massive buttes surrounded by this very minute object creates a visual poem dedicated to scale and frame of reference.

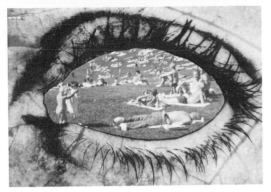

B&W A-35a, B-35b

We have tried to create a visual pun in the sharp contrast between this view of human environmental forms (sunning themselves in Oslo, Norway) and the previous scene of natural environmental forms. All these people, who look like they were having a very good time that day, are related quite closely to the plane on which they are reclining, sitting, or walking. Because of the nature of their activity, most of them are horizontal, a nice reiteration of the horizontality of this whole relief. The standing and sitting figures are projecting off the surface up into space in a scale that justifies calling this an environmental relief.

B&W A-36a, A-36b

In this University of Illinois student sculpture, the problem was to create an environmental relief that would harmonize with the architectural surround, which was itself an environmental relief. The handsome primary colors and bold geometry of the sculpture reflect the bricks of the building from which the artist derived his design. The black-and-white illustration shows the piece as a free-standing sculpture functioning in relation to the surround and to the surface plane on which both forms rest. If we could tip ourselves up and look down on the building from a couple of hundred feet, it would become part of a larger environmental relief composed of all the buildings in the area. The orientation of the plane in space is less important than the relative scale of the object in its surrounding environment.

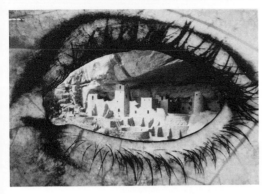

We have been noting all along as we talk about relief that its most important characteristic is that each plane of the form visually restates its debt to the bigger plane from which the forms rise or recede. The brilliantly lit facades of these Indian buildings at Mesa Verde, Colorado, which is an entire city carved out of a monolithic cliff face, are absolutely parallel to the plane of the cliff. This sculptured city, which bears a remarkable resemblance to European medieval villages, is one of the best examples, anywhere, of environmental relief. It is also a perfect illustration of three-dimensional figure-ground relationships, with convex and concave forms intertwined as if they were the jagged edges left by the bite a giant had taken out of the cliff in some bygone day. Is the cliff the positive or negative space? How would the dwelling appear if it were standing out in the middle of a plain? Black-and-white illustration A-37b shows a broader view of the entire cliff and the marvelous carved forms of this architectural environmental relief.

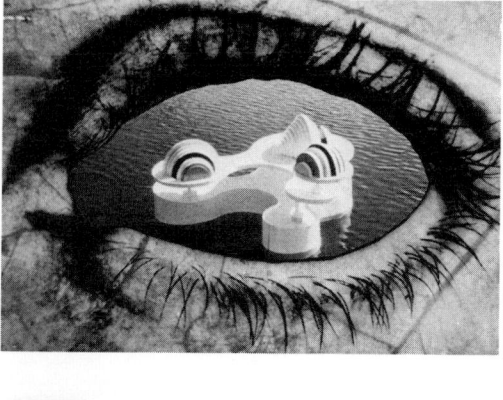

B&W A-38a, A-38b

Here is a very successful floating sculpture designed by a student to be in harmony with a large lake. As an environmental relief, it sensitively reflects the horizontal nature of the surface of the water, the flat plane it was designed to live in. The sculptor has anticipated the ripple pattern of the water by placing a series of concentric forms on the very top surface of the sculpture But at times winds come to force the thoughtful ripples, such as we have on this quiet summer day, into high waves. The bulging wavelike forms that sit on top of the horizontal plane of the sculpture imply these crests and troughs, these upward surges that occasionally disturb the surface of this changing environment.

B&W A-39a, A-39b

Colorful and serene as this cemetary in Taxco, Mexico, seems to be, it reflects one of the tragic aspects of Mexican life. The infant mortality rate is so high that parents set aside special areas as cemetaries for children who have died at an early age. In the black-and-white illustration we can study the horizontal and vertical planes of the shrines, how they are positioned in space, and how they reflect the lazy hill on which the cemetary is located. It is interesting to compare the scale effects of these miniaturized buildings, which appear in the photograph to be full-size houses, churches, and so on, with the full-size dwellings of Mesa Verde (A-37), which appear in their setting to be intricately formed doll's houses.

67

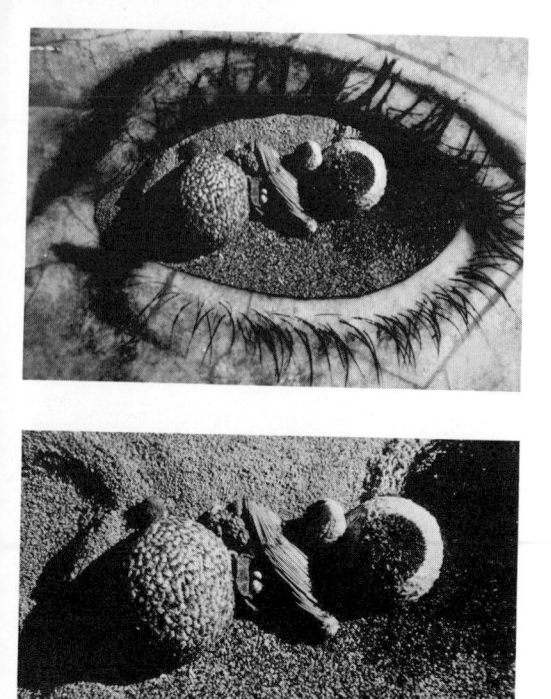

B&W A-40a, A-40b

This student sculpture is an environmental relief constructed of Styrofoam (plastic foam) covered with natural seeds, pods, stems, and twigs. All the nuances of relief are delicately manipulated here, with the seeds and weathering of the wood producing textured surfaces, and the smaller forms playing off against the larger ones in low and high relief. Rising from a gently modulated surface, which can be seen best in the black-and-white illustration, this classic example of environmental relief seems to reflect geological processes, as if the forms were being built up and torn down like mountains. The top of a round form is sliced off, producing a flat plane that repeats the ground plane. A cylinder emerges but is trapped by neighboring interfaces. A cluster of forms seems to evolve out of the plane into space, and the eye is invited to move from one form to another, forward and backward in space.

PART 2:
THREE-DIMENSIONAL DESIGN

TEXT TO STAGES 7-12, ROBERT FISHER

ANNOTATED CAPTIONS, STEWART KRANZ

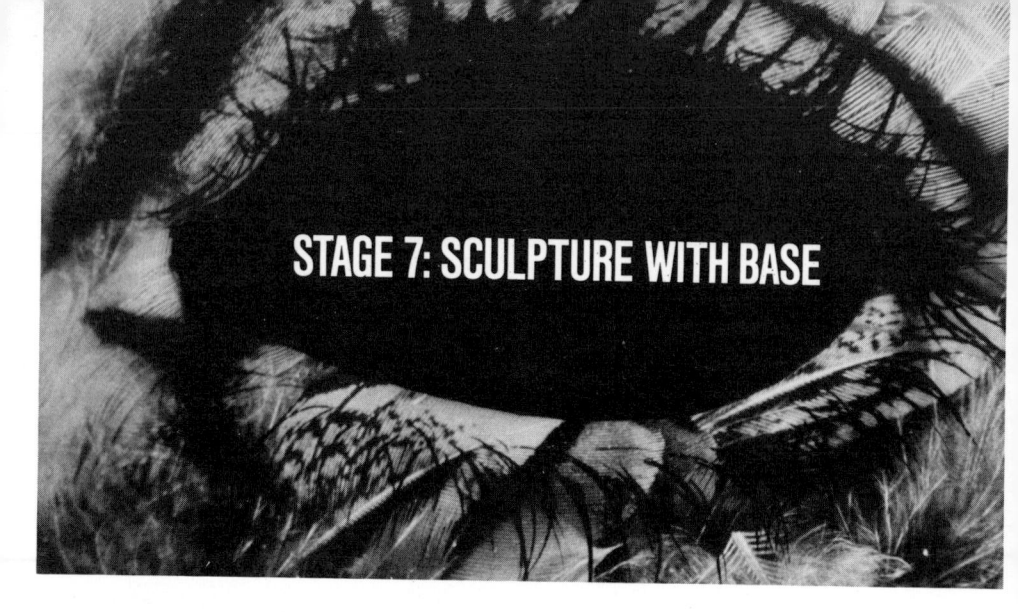

STAGE 7: SCULPTURE WITH BASE

CONCEPT

Sculptures with bases are emerging forms that have grown from the surface of an environmental relief to a position of further prominence. At the same time, the environmental surface shrinks and retracts until only a base is left, providing a subordinate but still key function in the total composition. A base is more than simply an appendage. It physically supports the mass and visually connects the mass to the material environment as a whole. The base is a pedestal or setting for the now dominant mass, a vital transition away from the unity with environment. Instead, it separates and displays the mass, offering many opportunities for visual exploration and meaning. In harmony or in contrast with that mass, the base is often as significant as the object which it cradles.

We are witness, at this stage in the continuum, to a significant transition point. The reduction of the *material* environment surrounding the mass signals a growth in the *spatial* environment surrounding the mass. In other words, as a mass becomes less reliant on its physical environs, it becomes increasingly dependent on its spatial environs.

CONTEXT

Think of a cowboy hero on his horse. Decked out in silver buckles, leather, and fringe, our western wonder is all the more impressive because of his white-maned, prancing stallion.

In the same way, when a jeweler sets a gem into a ring or necklace, the precious stone takes on a life it never had before. It has been made the center of attraction by the subtle design of the setting, which serves as its environment and has been created to emphasize the jewel's qualities. This base is often in itself an object of considerable beauty, made of precious metals and elaborately constructed.

In Italy, there now lives a designer-architect named Carlos Scarpa, who spent most of his efforts on the design of museums. First he remodelled and restored the ancient *palazzi*, or palaces, that served as environments for the works of art. Then he took each rare piece back to his studio in Venice and created an individual support for it, a base which emphasized the form and character of the work and acted as a perfect visual transition between it and the museum environment. These bases were often as beautiful or more beautiful than the objects they displayed. Taken together, the objects, their bases, and the environments created complex and total works of art.

APPROACHES AND MATERIALS

Select a found object that you like very much and wish to display to others. Design a base which emphasizes the best aspects of the object.

Construct a cubic or rectangular solid of Styrofoam (plastic foam), wood, or construction board. Paint it a primary color. Now design a base for your piece of minimal art which will make it as exciting to look at as possible. Cast a form in plaster in a balloon. Now create a base which will blend as harmoniously as possible with the form. Now create one that will contrast as much as possible.

Design a piece of jewelry for your hand. How does it relate to your fingers or wrist? Design a piece of furniture which looks like you belong in it. Let the furniture reflect your personality.

CAPTION NOTES

In the design continuum, we are concentrating on the evolution of form. We have already studied the emergence of three dimensions from a flat surface, and now, in the first stage of Part 2, we are going to concentrate on three-dimensional form that is independent of its environment, form that is taking on a life of its own. Throughout the second part of our design continuum we will be studying examples in which the environment is of less significance than the nature of the form that has emerged from it.

Because of the nature of the continuum, it is useful to make comparative evaluations of the stage under discussion with the stage that immediately precedes it, in this case Environmental Relief from Part 1 of the continuum, and the stage which follows it, Monolithic Mass. The black-and-white illustrations from these three stages show a progression of forms in relation to the environment, from object with environment (image A-34) to object with base (image B-3) to object alone (image B-10). In the environmental relief from Monument Valley, the form is firmly in relation to its ground plane. In the Mexican pyramid, the base is firmly in relation to its ground plane. In the Mexican pyramid, the base is treated as a transitional element between the supporting plane and the form, which seems to dominate the base. The base, however, cannot be dismissed as an extraneous element, as it reflects or complements the form that rises from it. In the Venezuelan Pavilion, a completely dominant form with no subordinate base is finally independent of the environment.

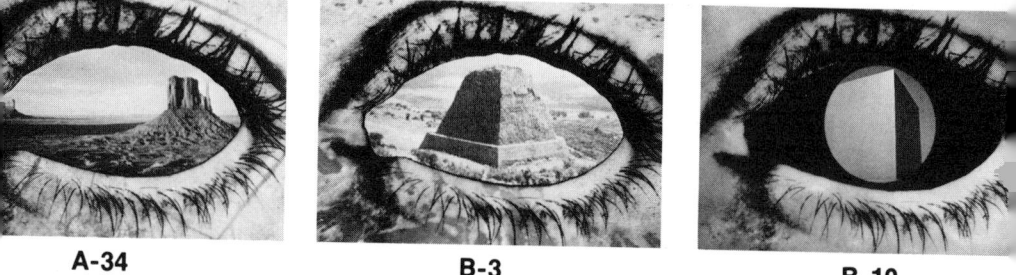

A-34   B-3   B-10

Taking a moment to examine the difference between these forms, we discover that it lies in part in the scale of the form in relation to the position of the observer, something we have had occasion to discuss in Part 1. The environmental relief would certainly qualify as sculpture with a base if viewed at closer proximity. But the monolithic mass would not. It is a huge cube, self-contained and self-defined, which could be placed anywhere in its environment without altering its essential characteristics.

B&W B-1a

This title image for the entire two-part *Understanding Visual Forms* introduces the basic format we have used throughout the set, in which a photograph of a human eye frames the visual area. The background of the Eye will be different in each stage of the continuum to provide a varying frame of reference for the student works. The black-and-white illustration of this image is numbered B-1a. The rest of the images will be composites, and black-and-white illustrations of each of the components will also be reproduced. From here on, we will call these study photographs "black-and-white illustrations."

Students of photography may be interested to know that the final visual image on the photos was created with an unusual technique of rear and front-screened projection, using extensive mattes of positive and negative areas, as well as double, triple, and quadruple superimpositions. Later images will show this in more detail. To create these effects as a classroom project requires two, three, and four slide projectors. The surround and the Eye area both need black Kodalith mattes so the projectors projecting on the screen will not wash out the visual image in either the surround or the Eye area.

B&W B-2a

This title image for *Part 2: Two Dimensional Design* uses a double projection, one for the eyelashes and eyebrows of the Eye, and the second for the surround area. Two projectors were used to create this effect. The central area is shown in full in the black-and-white illustration. The simple playoff between background and figure areas is expanded in the followng images, which form the illustrations proper for the seventh stage of our continuum.

B&W B-3a, B-3b

In the seven images of this stage of the continuum we are going to zoom our lens in on three-dimensional form, and study it almost without real concern, for the moment, with the environment that it lives in. Many architectural constructions have these qualities, creating their own environmental settings by the bases from which they rise. We have already begun our discussion of this clear example of sculpture with base. The form, a partially restored pyramid in Mexico, is essentially sculptural but emerges from a base which complements it and separates it from the environmental plane.

The Eye surround for this stage creates a most interesting contrast. It is a very close view of the bubbles in sea foam, and from our vantage point its contrasting values almost give it the appearance of a modulated ground plane, with slight projections and indentations. Visually it provides a flat environment from which the sculptures in the Eye can rise, while intellectually it serves as a reminder that the vantage point of the viewer is very important in classifying three-dimensional forms.

B&W B-4a, B-4b, B-4c

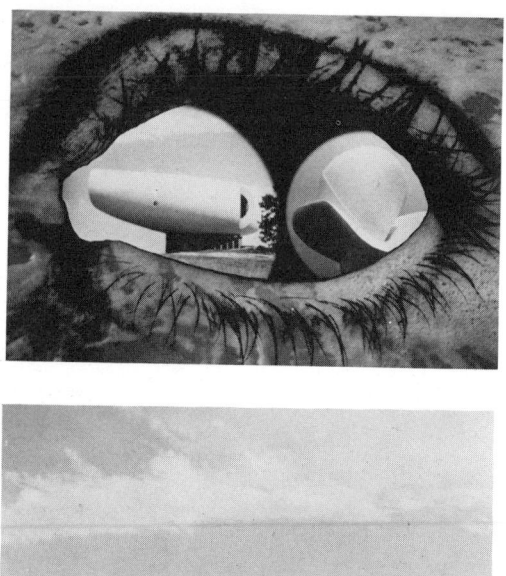

A close similarity between two functionally diverse structures shows that, essentially, the difference between sculptural and architectural form is a matter of scale. On the left, is a home designed by Colorado architect Charles Deaton. The base is secondary, almost incidental. In the black-and-white illustration of the house in its mountain top environment, with two splendid pine trees nearby, one can see that the form clearly dominates its base. In the student project of cast and carved plaster the cradle-like form of the base plays an important role, seeming to care for the egg-shaped sculpture. The base allows for and adequately predicts the organic character of the sculpture itself. Plaster, the material for this project, is an excellent choice at this stage of the continuum because it is an additive medium. The sculptor comes close to the volume he wants by molding and then with careful manipulating of the surface, brings it to the desired polish and final form.

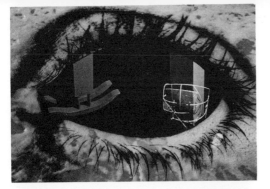

B&W B-5a, B-5b, B-5c

On the left, painted wood and cardboard create a nonfunctional form that was the solution to a problem of creating a base for a rectangular solid. The student artist makes the base runners relate to the main form by using support columns about six inches high that allow air to enter the area between base and rectangle. Because the supports are at the four corners of a rectangle, they hint at the dominant form in the sculpture. The other project, created from cardboard and soldered brass rods, again makes an inconsistent base work with a dominant form. The open linear pattern of rods does a whimsical levitation act with the rectangle. It is surrealist, almost a Paul Klee cartoon in tone.

B&W B-6a, B-6b, B-6c

These two tombstones point up the difference between sculpture with a base and the evolutionarily earlier stage of environmental. relief. In sculpture with a base, the mass of the sculpture dominates and holds our attention, as it does here with two folk-art carvings evocative of loneliness and grief. The dog's tombstone was photographed near Boothbay Harbor, Maine, and the woman's figure marks a grave near Central City, Colorado. The unembellished markers that can be seen in the background of both pictures are more obviously environmental reliefs because the forms are subordinate in scale to the environment. However, there are no sharp dividing lines between these stages of the continuum, and the difference is a matter of emphasis.

B&W B-7a, B-7b

This handsome sculpture grew out of a challenge to the student to create a base for a plaster form. He came up with a soldered welding-rod nest of linear shapes that cradles and encircles a strong sculptural volume. The open base, or net, allows us to see the dominant mass of the scupture. In the black-and-white illustration we can see how the harsh base lines, with their open protruding pieces of wire, create an aesthetic antithesis to the sensuous plaster form. Comparing this project with the rectangular form in B-5 shows how much the organic shaping here has added to the effect of contrasting materials. Such a tactile difference between metal and soft molded form has classically been profoundly exciting to the spectator. It is the same antithesis which increases the sensual character of a nude when it is adorned with necklaces, waist ornaments, or ankle bracelets.

Two immensely different "solutions" to the problem of creating sculpture with a base are shown in this comparison between a magnificent thunderhead that rises 30,000 or 40,000 feet in the air and an ingenious student who is himself the sculpture. The black-and-white illustrations help us explore these two unusual sculptures. The photograph of the cloud formation was taken in the Mexican plateau just south of Monterrey, in a late afternoon light. We have a form, infinitely larger than the highest mountain, rushing into the upper atmosphere. The sculpture, in this case the cloud, is resting on a column of heated air that is still close to the earth. As the warm air rushes up into the thin upper atmosphere, it mushrooms out into this bold natural form. On a more human scale, a student created his own costume and then stood on a base to create a sculptural form out of his own figure. It is a rich and original concept that again indicates the wide diversity of solutions possible in this stage of the design theory.

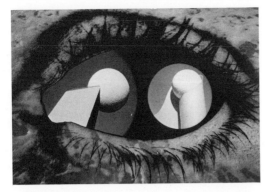

B&W B-9a, B-9b, B-9c

As we arrive at these last two dramatic examples of sculpture with a base, it should be clear that we are opening up a vast aesthetic playground when we focus our concern on individual forms rather than on forms in an environment, In the student project on the left, made of painted Styrofoam (plastic foam) and cardboard, the rectangular base lightly touches the crowning globe; in the student project on the right, made of painted Styrofoam and formed metal, a graceful column cradles the sphere. In each of these elegant examples, a balance has been achieved between base and sculptured object. Something close to a stasis is created, where the base has an important if not equal role in the total form.

With the twelve examples in this stage, we have made the transition from the primarily architectural concerns of environmental relief to features that are common to both sculpture and architecture. Sculpture with a base provides an important opportunity to experiment with different styles and aesthetics before turning to purely three-dimensional form in monolithic mass, which is the next stage and the focal point of the entire continuum.

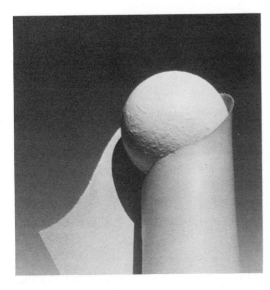

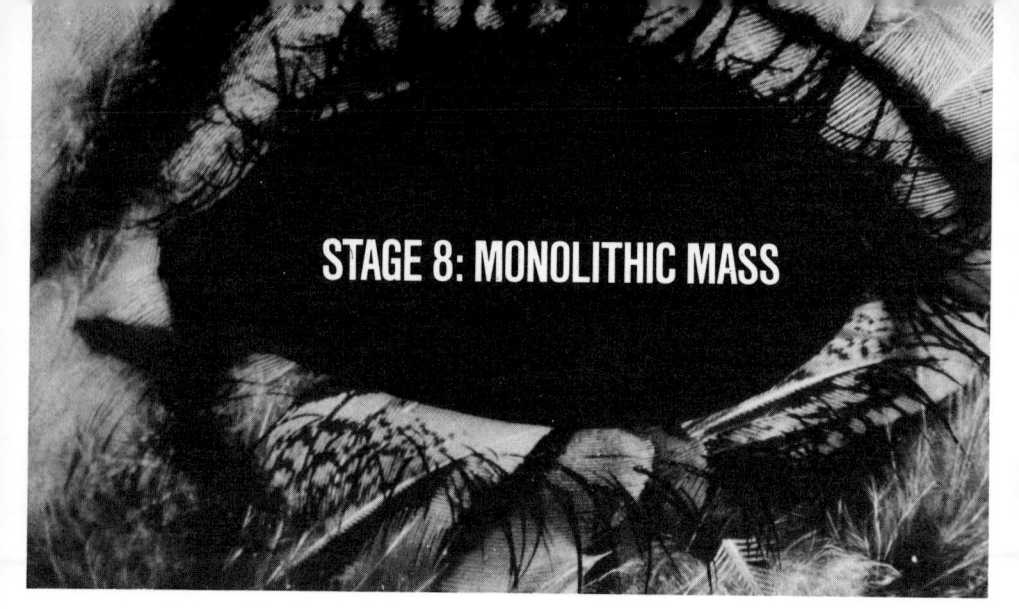

STAGE 8: MONOLITHIC MASS

CONCEPT

Defiant, resisting any intrusions by space into its surface, monolithic mass celebrates its independence by ignoring the rest of the material and spatial world. Gone forever is the material environment, the bases, the reliefs that once supported the object. The monolith is now alone in the emptiness of space like an astronaut.

At this stage we have completed one turn of our spiral continuum: from the empty plane of flat two-dimensional surfaces, unaffected by space, we have watched form evolve upward to a monolithic mass, again unaffected by space. Monolithic mass is the three-dimensional equivalent of a flat plane.

But the spiral turns back on itself, and the pressures of space will begin to work their invisible magic once again. How long can these pressures be resisted by perfect monolithic mass? Alas, the future looks grim. The forces of space are lining up for the battle to be played out in the remaining stages of the continuum.

CONTEXT

Any essentially smooth, solid form is a monolithic mass. From an ice cream cone to a can of beer, from an ice cube to a grapefruit, from the pyramid of Cheops to a loaf of bread, monolithic masses sit everywhere in our daily lives. Tree trunks, locker trunks, the Washington Monument, basketballs, Easter eggs, quarts of milk—the monolithic mass is common because it is efficient. Its interface is an effortless resolution of inner and outer forces. Next time you drive past one of those futuristic-looking petroleum storage tanks in the shape of a huge metal sphere, consider the physics of the situation more closely. The gas which it contains pushes outward with even pressure all around, while the rigid surface of the sphere traps the gas evenly; the pressures are the same at every point.

Packaging is a wide concept. Petroleum processors package their product in storage tanks, food processors package chickens or vegetables in cans or boxes, fruit trees package their seeds in apples, pears, plums, or peaches. These varying monolithc containers have come to be used because they work. So too, the rectangular solids of skyscrapers package offices and apartments most effectively, and the geometric objects of minimalist sculptures package the purest feeling of solidity.

APPROACHES AND MATERIALS

Look at a reproduction of Michelangelo's slaves struggling to liberate themselves from the uncarved block. Feel the resistance to space suggested by monolithic masses. Now start with a solid, hard substance like wood or concrete, and chip, grind, and chisel the form into being.

Study the work of Brancusi and the charming and evocative Eskimo soapstone sculptures. Notice how the solids have been modified as little as possible, with only a few intrusions or cavities suggesting the form. Now cast plaster of Paris into a balloon or waxed cardboard container. Before it dries completely, carve the plaster with a knife. After it is dry, use a rasp, then files, and finally sandpaper to finish the subtractive sculpture.

CAPTION NOTES

Monolithic mass is the most easily recognized stage of the continuum. You simply cannot argue about an object that is totally self-contained. The last vestiges of a base are discarded and the solid three-dimensional form emerges as a total and self-defining entity. A monolithic mass is a closed, independent form into which nothing intrudes, either physically or visually, although the mass is completely surrounded by the environment. Sometimes it is merely a thin skin surrounded by space both inside and outside, like a balloon. It is the closed independent form that makes an object a monolithic mass, no matter how solid it really is, or what it's size may be, relative to the environment.

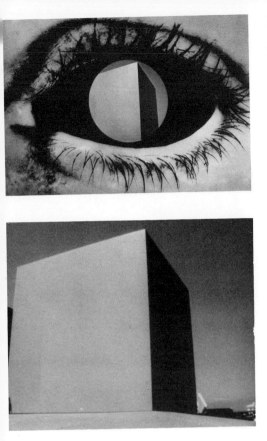

B&W B-10a, B-10b

We have already used this dramatic contemporary building, the Venezuelan Pavilion from Expo '67 in Montreal, Canada, in our comparison with the Mexican pyramid with a base (B-3) from Stage 7. The Pavilion's uninterrupted mass stands absolutely independent of its environment, like a piece of sculpture, even though it is a functional piece of architecture. Try to imagine the building in a desert, on a mountain, or in a forest. No matter how the environment changes, the monolithic quality of the form will endure.

The Eye surround for the six images of this stage of the continuum is a photograph of the blue sky with several wispy clouds in it. With this version of empty space we are attempting to set the pieces shown within the Eye free from any surrounding environment in order to reinforce our point that monolithic masses function as fully independent three-dimensional forms.

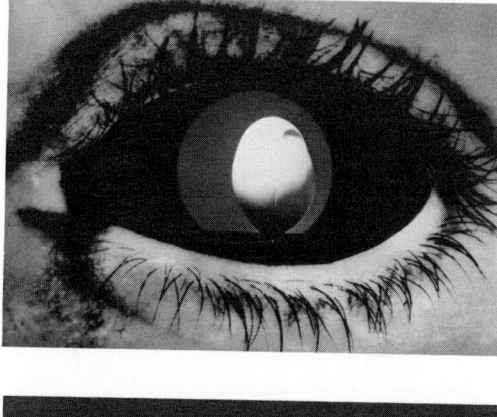

B&W B-11a, B-11b

No matter how large or small a monolithic form may be physically, it will always appear massive and powerful when viewed in a neutral environment. The very nature of the shape creates that response. The closed convex surfaces required of monolithic forms lend themselves naturally to pure geometric shapes. Here, in a student project of cast and carved plaster, we have an egg-like form with the slightest hint of deformation of the surface, which only adds by contrast to the solidity of the total effect. In the next stage of the continuum, Concave-Convex Mass, we will see what happens when space enters deeper into the impenetrable fullness of monolithic mass.

B&W B-12a, B-12b

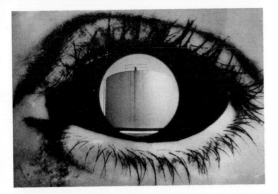

We have chosen a steel storage tank photographed in Illinois as an example of monolithic mass because it is such a familiar form throughout the United States. It has all the essential qualities we are looking for, namely, that it is convex, self-contained, and impenetrable. It is instructive to compare the black-and-white illustration of the tank in its environment with the black-and-white illustration of the tank in the Eye, where the environment has been effectively masked. The impression of form does not change at all, as we might expect, since one of the essential features of a monolithic mass is its aesthetic independence from the environment, a quality this tank very clearly illustrates.

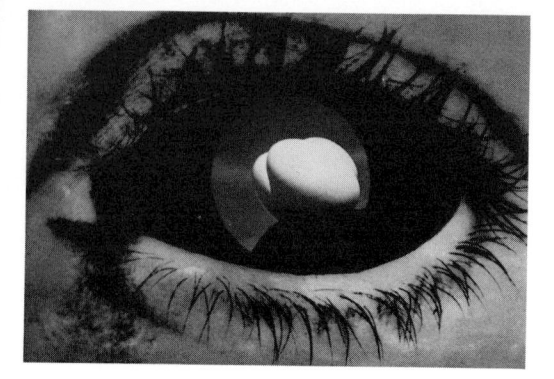

B&W B-13a, B-13b

Some modulation of a purely convex surface is acceptable at this stage, as long as it does not detract from the massive overall effect of the form. This is exactly the case here; a sensuous sculpture has been created with only a suggestion of less than totally unrelieved geometric shape. Compare the effect of the single large indentation in this form with the two small concavities in the egg-shaped student sculpture (B-11). Each piece maintains the integrity of the three-dimensional form by suggesting that the space around it is not able to essentially change the nature of the object.

B&W B-14a, B-14b

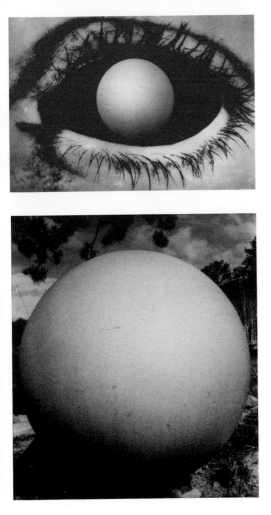

Here is monolithic form in its purest geometric sense, a totally unrelieved sphere. At first glance, it is possible to tell what we are dealing with, but when we see it in its environment in the black-and-white illustration we discover with surprise that this is a massive storage tank near Fort Collins, Colorado. Even then, we can hardly believe it. The unrelieved shape so dominates the environment by form and scale that it seems to have no functional relation to it, as if it were a mysterious object left by visitors from another planet.

This sphere is a complete expression of the concept under discussion. We might consider it as the apex of the whole continuum, in the sense that all the stages before monolithic mass show three-dimensional form slowly evolving out of the environment, and all the stages after monolithic mass will show the reintegration of the environment within the form. Only at this stage, as shown so clearly by this example, are the form and the environment completely separated.

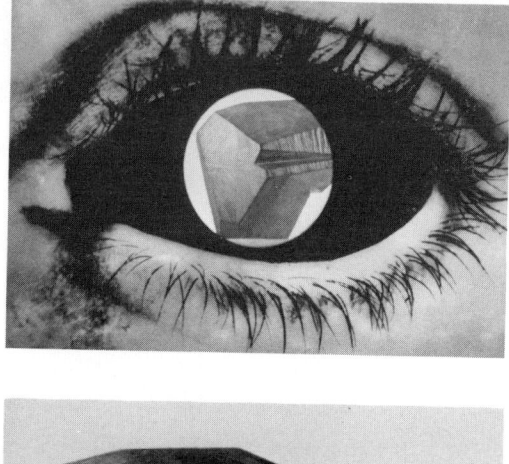

B&W B-15a, B-15b

We conclude our discussion of monolithic mass with this excellent carved soapstone sculpture. It is a student project on a small scale, with a height not much over six inches, yet the powerful shape makes it seem to be a massive rock formation. To understand how the effect was achieved in such a small piece will state the heart of our concept about monolithic form. The shape is closed, the surfaces are smooth, the planes are relatively large in relation to the total volume. Where indentations occur, they either break the form into separate self-contained areas (as in B-13) or change the plane only slightly in relation to the total shape, as if the solidity of the form stopped them short. Material is an aid in creating this illusion of massiveness; we are accustomed to thinking of rock formations as being very large. Soft-looking surfaces, such as the dull lavender metal of the round storage tank in B-14 give us less of an illusion of great size. Perhaps this is why the huge scale of the tank and the tiny scale of this stone carving are both so startling.

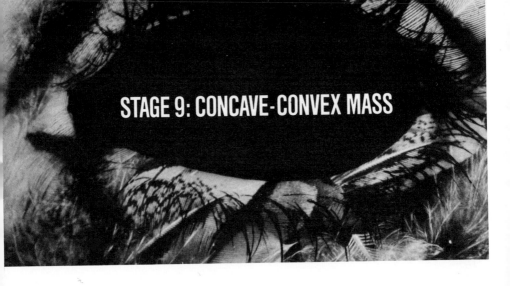

STAGE 9: CONCAVE-CONVEX MASS

CONCEPT

While the first portion of the design continuum described the growth of form from a plane to a solid mass, the second phase of the continuum defines the dissolution of form into space. The deterioration of the monolithic mass proceeds as a three-dimensional parallel to the earlier stages of textured surfaces, low relief surfaces, and high relief surfaces.

Concave-Convex mass is the first indication of what direction this change will take. Space has penetrated the mass from the outside, forming concavities, and consequently pushed aside part of the mass, forming convexities. The swellings and indentations suggest forces at work on the visual form from both inside and outside. The interface of the mass first reacted to the slight pressures of space with ripples and small bumps of texturing. Then larger concavities appear, with light catching their outer curves and casting shadows in their hollows. The entire form softens in the process, as if space had found its weak spots, and begins its reintegration with the environment.

CONTEXT

Did you ever squeeze a piece of fruit to see if it was solid, and have your fingers sink in about half an inch, leaving deep impressions in the soft surface? You had just created your first concave-convex mass.

Look at the form of a bird in flight, of an animal asleep, of a pumpkin at rest in your garden. See how the modelling of light passing over the curves in the forms gives you an impression of yielding softness. So too, does that big soft pillow chair you curl up in, the apple you took a bite out of, your catcher's mitt, your car, and your bottle of Coke. All of these objects seem responsive to our touch because they represent monolithic masses that have yielded to the touch of space.

No matter what the concave-convex mass is made of, one is reminded of living things, whose organic structures have evolved by yielding to the necessities of inner growth and outer restraint. The human face, shaped from within by the bony skull and its openings and from without by the wind, weather, and storms of life, offers a superb example of concave-convex mass. Claes Oldenburg, with his contemporary soft sculptures of vacuum cleaners and catcher's mitts, and Edward Weston, with his photographs of cabbage leaves, shells, and peppers, have portrayed the organically sensual qualities of concave-convex mass so strongly that we sometimes think we are looking at details of the human form.

APPROACHES AND MATERIALS

Study Egyptian sculpture. Now, starting with a solid mass of clay, begin to suggest the human form by scraping away at the surface, not too deep, just enough to catch the light. Create a suggestion of roundness, a suggestion of arms, legs, and neck. Now go a little further. Take the monolithic mass you spent so much time smoothing out in the last stage of the continuum and dig into its surface. Spoon out some caves, roughen its texture, pretend you are space and the solidity of mass is your enemy.

That was subtractive sculpture. Conversely, begin with a block of wood or shoe box or plastic bottle. Collect many small found objects such as nuts, bolts, buttons, seeds, nuts, golf tees, cookies, cereal, and sea shells. Glue these to the surface of the mass in a continuous relief. Now paint the object white or black or any solid color. Then use the surface to inspire color. Create a three-dimensional relief painting and call it additive sculpture.

Make another form out of found objects. Then take cloth and wrap the form like a mummy, smoothing out the deep depressions, leaving only an implication of what lies beneath the surface. Is this a subtractive or additive way of creating a concave-convex mass?

CAPTION NOTES

Concave-convex mass marks the beginning of reintegration of environment with three-dimensional form. There is a sense of interaction between the two, shown in hollow depressions within the general closed surface. And these concavities deform the surface convexity so that the object is no longer a self-defining monolithic mass. To define concave-convex mass we must describe both object and environment, or, as we will call it in the following descriptions, positive and negative space. Positive space is dominant at this stage, though in later stages we will see more and more negative space reentering the form until it has reduced positive area to a three-dimensional linear structure.

In a way you might say that concave-convex mass is a three-dimensional figure-ground relationship. What we call negative, that is the background area, could just as well be called positive if one conceives of the form as an interlinking network of empty space penetrated by solidity.

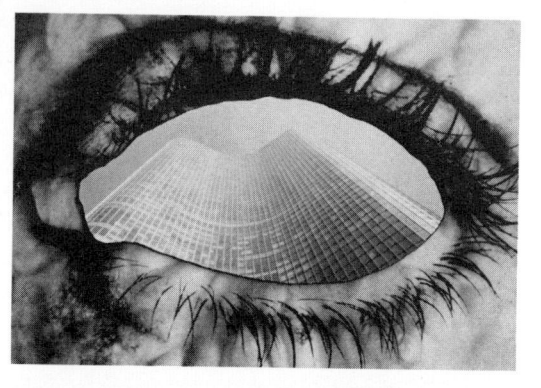

B&W B-16a, B-16b

A skyscraper apartment on Lake Shore Drive in Chicago is an impressive introduction to our new stage of the design continuum. We are drawn into its undulating facade; it seems to fling its sides out in a gesture of welcome. From this feeling of receptiveness we realize that the negative space has begun to change the essential definition of the form. It is no longer independent and impenetrable, although its monumental quality has not been impaired.

The Eye surround for this stage of the continuum seems to be a close-up view of a delicious summer squash whose rhythmic surface has produced undulations and swellings by growing according to the rules of its own nature. As a background for the six images in this stage, it serves to remind us how frequently concave-convex masses of metal, wood, plastic or other inert materials reflect the shapes of life itself.

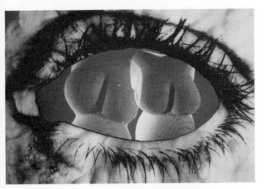

B&W B-17a, B-17b, B-17c

This student project, a rich wood carving of concave-convex masses, can be viewed as an abstract movement of shapes that swell outward while space presses them back. But the temptation is irresistible to see it as a female torso. No longer is the form a monolithic geometric solid; a few simple indentations on simple rounded forms have produced a totally different impression.

We have chosen to present two views of the wood carving in different orientations and lighting to show how light and shadow create dramatic effects on these masses, much as they did in the two-dimensional stages of low and high relief. The only essential difference between a relief and a concave-convex mass is that a relief is structurally and visually dependent on the two-dimensional plane from which it rises. The small area of overlapping in this image provides a visual example of how positive space can become negative space, depending on one's frame of reference. Here the shoulder of the form on the left, which is positive space when viewed from its own standpoint, becomes a shadowy intrusion, a negative area, when seen in relation to the form on the right. The overlapping within the Eye shows more clearly than in the matted images how we used the technique of double projection to create our collage effects.

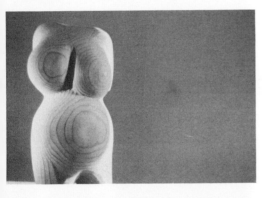

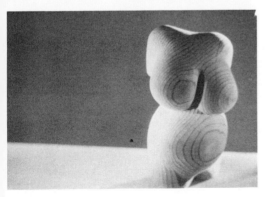

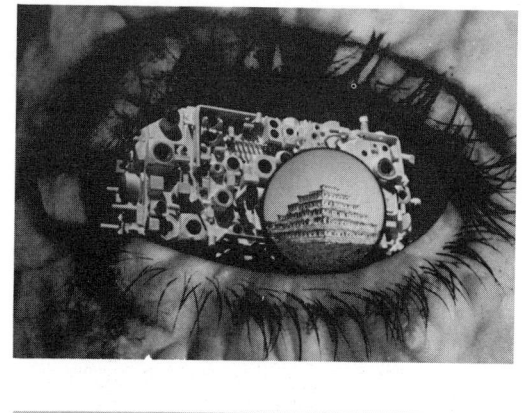

B&W B-18a, B-18b

Concave-convex mass need not be created from rounded areas, it can be angular and sharp-edged. Both of our examples here are strong geometric shapes permitting little interference with their essential positive mass, yet are not monolithic because the areas of negative space are too widespread. One piece is a student project of found objects such as nuts and washers, which have been glued to a wooden form and painted. The other is a pyramid called El Tajin, in Mexico. The windowed galleries that line the face of the pyramid open it up to negative space, producing a decorative frailty as if the piece were a three-dimensional low relief. It is interesting to compare the complexity of the negative space in the first three examples we have shown at this stage. In the skyscraper in B-16, one simple but enormous negative area modulates the entire solid; in the wood carving in B-17, several smaller indentations mold forms out of a convex surface; and in the present two examples, an intricate network of shallow penetrations changes the surfaces but not the geometrical outlines of the forms.

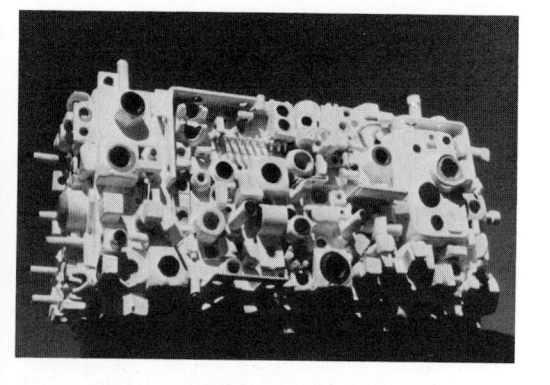

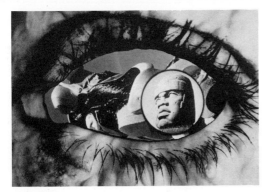

B&W B-19a, B-19b, B-19c

In this image we see a polychromed student sculpture, a composition of shoes and other found objects that had been superimposed on a wood block and then painted. This is contrasted with the jaguar head from Jalapa, Mexico, that we studied as a detail in Part 1. There the projections seemed to rise off an essentially flat plane, providing an excellent example of relief form. It is fair enough to use a full shot here as an example of concave-convex mass, showing the beginnings of penetration of space into the positive mass. This monumental head is subtractive sculpture because the huge piece of stone has been carved down to the form we see. The student piece is an additive sculpture, though still a concave-convex mass, with a core on which objects are imposed and literally bent to the will of the artist.

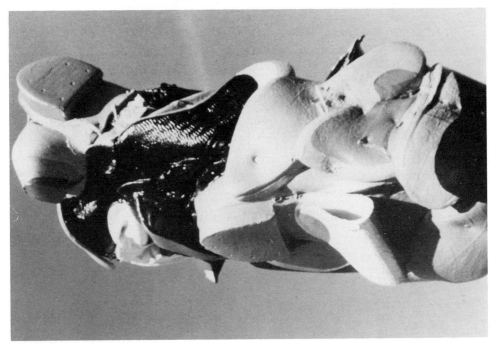

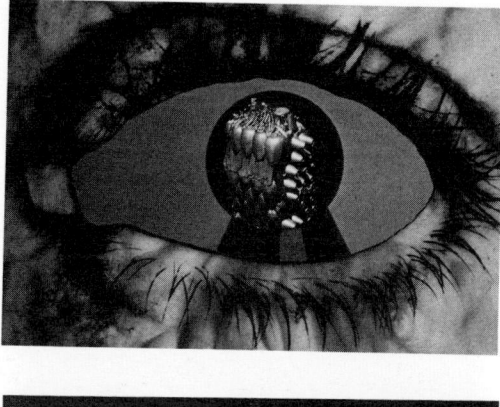

B&W B-20a, B-20b

An ingenious use of a variety of found objects such as nails, spoons, and gears is illustrated in this detail of a student sculpture. Again the found objects were glued to a wood block and painted. The black-and-white illustration shows the full sculpture, and makes it clear that convexities have been used to swell the sides and top of the sculpture outwards into space, while concavities produce deep indentations in the front. The differential use of these two methods of building form produces a very convincing illusion that the piece is actually made in two parts, an inner core and an outer sheath.

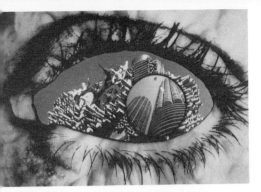

B&W B-21a, B-21b

In this last unlikely comparison, this time between a student sculpture of found objects on wood and the Marina Tower Apartments located in Chicago, we see the final result of the intrusion of negative space on positive form. In the remarkable apartment complex, which can be seen fully with its supporting ramps in the black-and-white illustration, the entire surface of the powerful mass is eroded with space. Nothing remains of the positive volume but its outline and a series of stacked planes, fluted columns and half-cookie-like terraces. We see much the same thing in the student example, where the negative space has left empty tubes and columns like guns on a tank. If the space were to go any further into either of these forms it would go right through them, which is exactly the case in our next stage of the continuum.

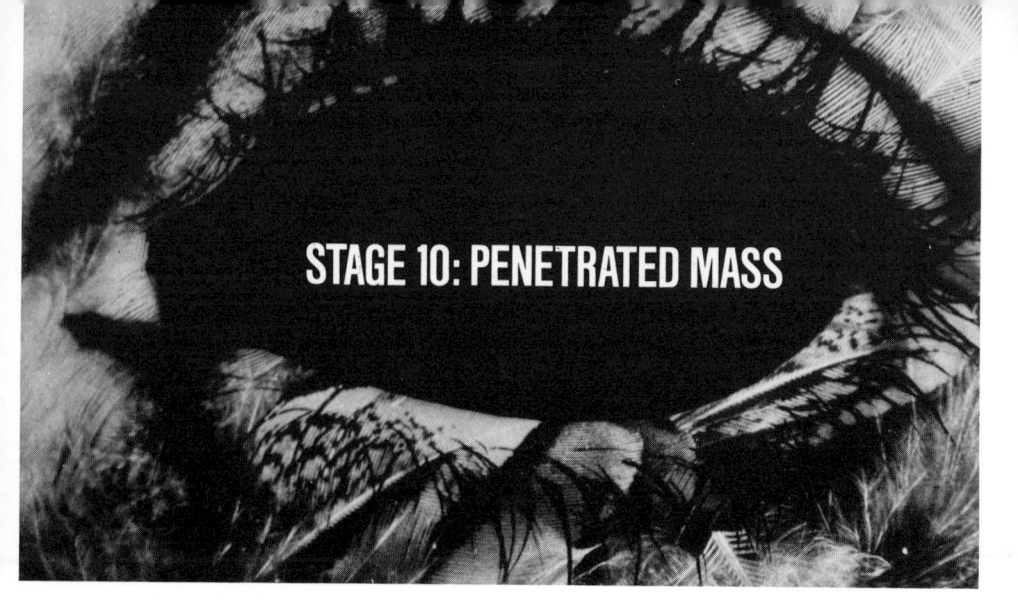

STAGE 10: PENETRATED MASS

CONCEPT

Relentlessly, space pursues its collision course with mass, and mass succumbs yet again. Great caves and holes take shape, adding depth and mystery to the interface. These are caves that lead the eye into the innermost regions of mass, and holes that permit vision clear through to the other side. Suddenly mass assumes more meaning, for the very space that destroyed solidity, poking and prodding at the surface, now sweeps in and over, around and through, touching inside with outside, front with back, left side with right side. Perceptual connections are made, and we conceive of mass for the first time as existing suspended within space, like a fish in water.

Strange bedfellows, mass and space. In penetrated forms they have intertwined and become inseparable companions. But even this equilibrium is temporary, for soon the balance will be tipped toward space, as mass withdraws further into itself, becoming a sea of holes.

CONTEXT

Like a railroad car with sleeping compartments, penetrated mass suggests forms in which space rests comfortably within the mass. In fact, most of the complex machines we see in workshops, with their strong projections, tables, handles, and tracks, are excellent examples of this stage of the continuum.

Much contemporary architecture combines the effect of massive concrete slabs with uninhibited open space. Mass and space act in consort in these structures, both framing and freeing the movement of life within the form. In the past, too, spatial openings set off the massive Greek columns, lent an effect of floating lightness to the dome of the Hagia Sophia, revealed a strong sense of proportion in the defined courtyards of Renaissance palaces, and became the dominant visual element in Gothic and Japanese architecture.

In other cases, space swirls around and cuts fluidly into the mass, like the strange eroded rock forms of Western landscapes. The vast majority of figurative sculpture, beginning long ago with early Greek statues, can be characterized by the relation of the solid torso and head to the open spaces created by the limbs. The sculptors have consciously emphasized these openings to greater or lesser degree. There are examples of architecture too, as in the rounded shapes and decorations of Baroque buildings, where space and mass curl into each other like waves crashing on a craggy shore.

APPROACHES AND MATERIALS

Study the voids that remain when rough-shaped forms inter-weave with one another. Take chunks of wood and mass them to-gether. Add or subtract: space from mass, mass from space. Layer space on space with thick slabs of wood. Pile found ob-jects on one another. Paint them so the composition becomes a new object. Create an architectural statement for a city.

Walk in the woods and then echo the rotted stumps, the mushroom clusters, the piles of abandoned rusted metal and other man-made objects. Cast a plaster mass and bore through it. Laminate a block of wood and turn it into a bowl or handle or complex form. Carve plastic foam with files, wire brushes, and sandpaper until it becomes as smooth as water-formed rock.

Place a light within the openings of one of your forms. Con-ceal it so only the rays of light emit from within. Sense the flow of space as light, as water. Create a playground for fish, for children. Use tires and other found, penetrated forms to encour-age the child, like a wandering eye, to explore the innermost reaches of mass.

CAPTION NOTES

Penetrated mass is the next step in the interaction of form and space. As the negative space moves in from all sides it makes dark, mysterious pockets of indeterminate depth, and finally breaks through entirely, connecting one side to the other. The hole now becomes a shape within the sculpture, a physical part of the composition itself. Many sculptors and architects since classic times have deliberately worked with the negative form as part of their total design.

B&W B-22a, B-22b

This stage of the continuum finishes a smooth and comprehensible transition from monolithic mass, where negative space has no effects, to concave-convex and penetrated mass, where it progressively alters the form. As you look at this student project of cast and carved plaster, try a mental exercise: fill in the holes. Now you have a concave-convex form. It is almost as if the wind has worn away this shape over many years, naturally creating a balance of positive and negative areas.

The Eye surround for the seven images in this stage is an unusual penetrated mass, rock-like in its texture yet with organic protuberances and cavities. It is an enormously enlarged view of the underside of a crab, whose planes remind us of the largest of natural or man-made formations.

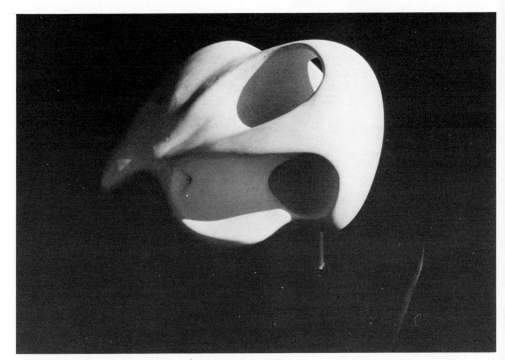

B&W B-23a, B-23b, B-23c

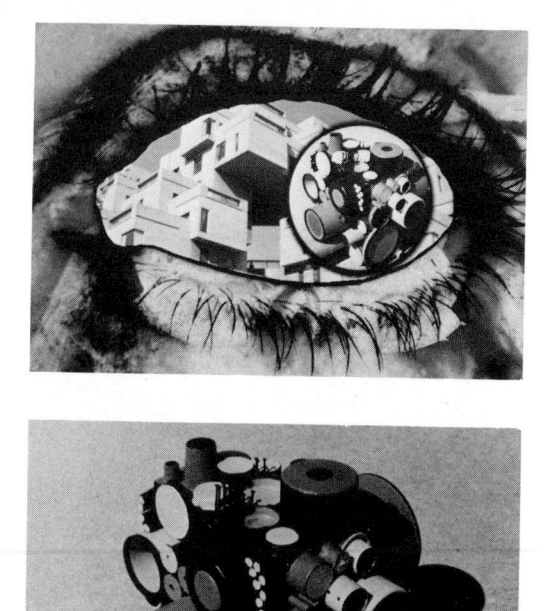

If we compare the painted cans and cardboard of this student project with the view of the Habitat Apartments in Montreal, Canada, we see that both are composed of a canon of forms carefully opposed to each other on a 90-degree axis. In the architectural piece the repeated modules are rectangles and squares and in the student piece they are cylinders and spheres. The positive definition of each of the shapes is nearly balanced by an opposing outline of negative space, somewhat like a lock and key. The whole of the Habitat Apartments, which can be seen in the black-and-white illustration, is assembled as if it were a Tinker Toy. Habitat was the sensation of Expo '67 in Montreal because it introduced the concept of modular construction into apartment dwelling, and later it became a coveted dwelling area for Montreal citizens. Each module is an independent entity, and, amazingly, no one living space looks into another living space.

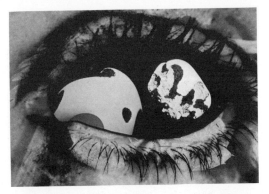

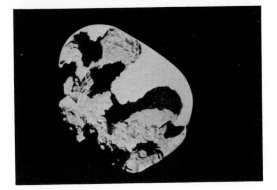

B&W B-24a, B-24b

Two views of one piece, a cast and carved plaster student project, show that sculpture can be deceptive. Viewed from one face, the positive, convex form has only small indentations of negative space, although we cannot immediately tell how deep these holes go. As we turn the piece over we see a terribly eroded surface, where the negative space assumes great importance by strongly suggesting the *absence* of positive form. Where did it go? Was it eaten away from the outside or did it explode from its very core? This is a brilliant student solution to the concept of penetrated mass.

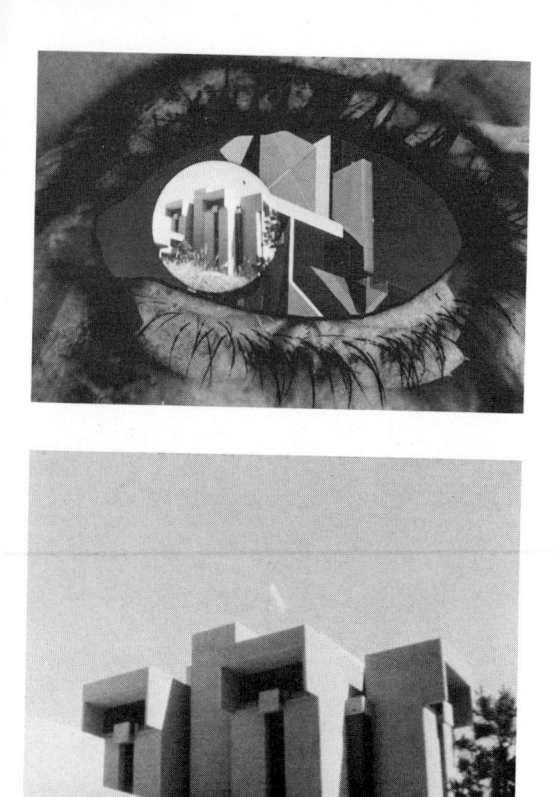

B&W B-25a, B-25b, B-25c

It should be clear by now that in this particular grouping of slides we are giving you a sort of visual shock therapy, moving back and forth from organic forms (B-22 and B-25) to geometrically penetrated forms (B-23). This geometric building, the National Center for Atmosphere, in Boulder, Colorado, was designed by the architect I. M. Pei. Instead of squares and rectangles as in Habitat, we now have stacked right-angled slices of positive form, which approach the planar forms we will be considering in the next stage of the continuum. The structural similarities to the student project on the right can be seen most clearly in the black-and-white illustrations. Different colors, particularly light and dark values, produce illusory movement in the wood planes of the sculpture and partially mask the play of positive and negative space.

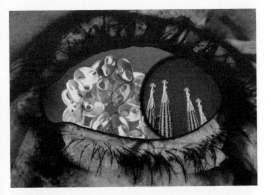

B&W B-26a, B-26b, B-26c

Back to organic form. We have side by side Gaudi's La Sagrada Familia Church in Barcelona, Spain, and a modular paper sculpture by a student. Antonio Gaudi, one of the geniuses of Spanish art, created almost single-handedly a body of work so unique that it is instantly distinguishable from the work of other architects. One of his strongest abilities was to open up a form to air, through almost Gothic filigree, and make it seem to float in space. In the student project, a paper module has been created and then formed into a handsome three-dimensional sculpture. The entire surface of the work is indented and embellished by negative space. Like the modular church spires, the units cannot be neatly classified by geometric form. They seem to have grown that way, like living things.

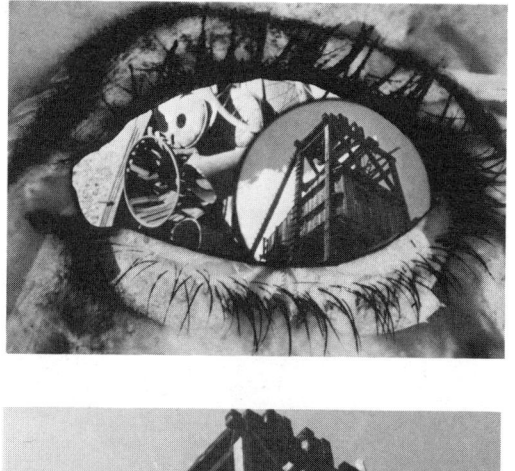

B&W B-27a, B-27b, B-27c

A silver-mine shaft in Leadville, Colorado, and a student assemblage of found junk tell us a great deal about what has happened to our concept of three-dimensional form. We can see the arrangement of positive areas more clearly in the black-and-white illustrations. Huge timber on the shaft, as well as a bicycle wheel's rim and spokes, merely enclose and define the areas of negative space. We are getting near the heart of the matter, close to what penetrated mass really means. The sense of stability and endurance in monolithic and concave-convex masses is hardly maintained here. Instead, there is a rather tentative arrangement of positive forms around an imposing element of space.

B&W B-28a, B-28b, B-28c

We now have a very handsome Victorian mansion in Galena, Illinois, compared to a student project of dolls' heads on a potty chair, a whimsical example of a solution to creating a form that balances precariously on the cliff of positive and negative space. In the mansion, the balconies and porches and window areas speak of a form literally opened up to negative space. The galleries, the wooden pillars and pilasters, the balcony railings, the high overhang of the gables all trap space, and as they do so, they invite us to meditate on how far from the monolithic aesthetic of the Venezuelan Pavilion (B-10) we have come in our continuum. As we shall see in the remaining two stages of our continuum, planar and linear three-dimensional forms, the movement of our analysis is toward a gentler hold of positive form on the negative space it controls, and a more ephemeral definition of the mass itself.

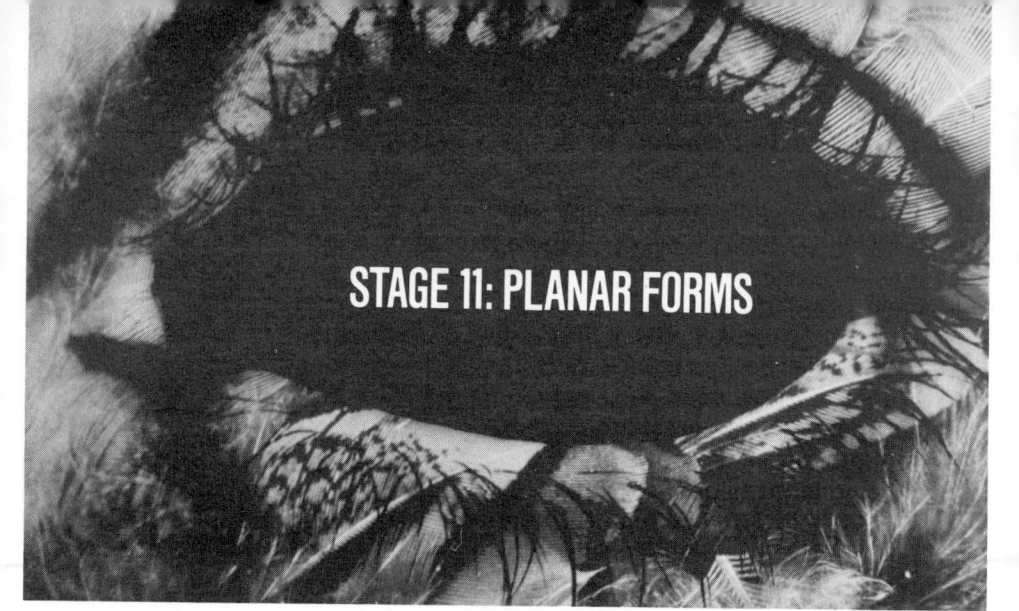

STAGE 11: PLANAR FORMS

CONCEPT

At this stage, mass does little more than serve as a guide to the flow of space through the form. Now reduced to a series of interlocking planes, mass shapes the passage of space, thrusting, compressing, expanding, and perforating. No solids stop the flow; only thin, wafer-like surfaces interrupt but do not hinder, suggest but do not demand, structure but do not enclose. Just as we sense the wind's real substance and presence when we watch a regatta of sailboats, so we can sense the presence of space in the shapes of planar forms.

Planar forms signal a return of an interface not unlike the earliest flat two-dimensional surface in this continuum. But several significant conceptual differences separate the two. First, the original plane had but one side, the front surface facing the viewer, while the planes in planar form are three-dimensional, that is, they have a front and a back. Then, too, the early surface was flat and did not interact at all with space, while planar three-dimensional surfaces can twist and bend, making forms as free as the wind.

CONTEXT

Spoons and plates, napkins and towels, shoes and sheet music, barns and basketball backboards, grave markers, frisbees, wings of airplanes, birds, and butterflies, sails on boats and kites, banners and flags, glassware and dishes, pots and pans, dollar bills and coins, sheet-metal ducts and duck's feathers—planar forms are so common, it is easy to see why our ancestors thought the earth was flat.

In nature the planar form is a sheath. The skins of snakes and the shells of creatures of the sea and land like clams, snails, cicadas, armadillos, and turtles, all reveal variations on a theme. Planar forms allow a maximum interaction with the environment, so they are the most efficient form for leaves on trees and shrubs, which must have maximum exposure to sun and air. They are the most efficient surfaces to serve us also, from caps for our teeth to contact lenses, from the very paper on which this is written to the desk, chairs, and windows of the room where it is read. From the most primitive tents to the ultramodern cantilevered buildings in our cities, architectural forms are often built around the airy structures of three-dimensional planes.

APPROACHES AND MATERIALS

Dip a cloth or other fabric in plaster. Drape it and let it harden. Now paint the folds and shadows. Sew a costume emphasizing the planes of the fabric. Make a dress or hat of cardboard or paper.

Take a branch, hoops, welded frame, or other linear structure and use it as a loom, weaving planes in the spaces out of yarns, rope, string, or wire. Bend and curve thin sheet metal, foil, and aluminum using tin snips, a hammer, and a block of wood to pound against. Now make a mobile, floating planes in space, or cantilever a plane off a wall using the structural system of leaves or wings. Create a stage set of planes, coloring them so that they accentuate the advancing and receding of the planes in space.

Study origami, the Japanese art of paper folding. Have a contest for the most unusual and flyable kite or paper airplane. Make a house of playing cards. Cut and glue construction board. Cut and fold paper into sculptured forms. Study the flow of space as it responds to the forms you create.

CAPTION NOTES

In the next two stages, planar and linear forms, the star of the show will be the man who isn't there—the power of negative space as it is defined by positive space.

In planar forms, a three-dimensional shell describes a volume created out of negative space. This volume cannot be entirely enclosed by the plane or visually it would become a monolithic mass. Think of a shell, however, in which the convolutions of the planar form suggest so much air that the object would seem fragile even if it were made of steel. That could never happen with an enclosed solid such as a balloon or a balloon-shaped storage tank. In terms of mass, a minimal quantity of planar material has been spread out in such a way as to dominate a maximum portion of the environment, which can generate exciting design problems in sculpture and architecture. The planes take on the role of space articulators, which serve to divide and mold space much as an architect considers the walls of his rooms.

B&W B-29a, B-29b

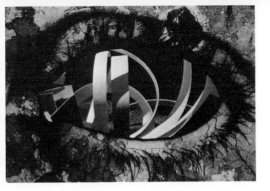

Here, in a student project of steamed and curved balsa wood, we see how a simple plane or series of planes in space can define a negative object. The swooping curves of the plane encircle and control the powerful void they encompass.

In the Eye surround for these six images we have returned to a simple flat plane, against which the curved surfaces of our planar forms arise. The photograph is of a lichen-encrusted rock, one of nature's most painterly productions.

B&W B-30a, B-39b, B-30c

We witness the architecture of planar form in these two juxtaposed examples which occupy a minimum of actual space but still make strong visual statements. In the student sculpture of laminated paper, a single plane has been bent around itself, and in the tropical leaf photographed in Mexico a single plane has been corrugated and gently modulated. Now if we look at the black-and-white illustrations we can see an interesting phenomenon. Our eyes are drawn immediately to any positive objects although they really occupy a very small amount of total space. Presumably this derives from the psychological need to defend one's own environmental space. We do not have to pay attention to the field, only to objects intruding on it.

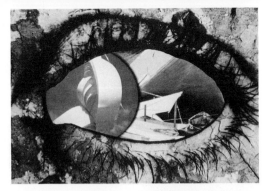

B&W B-31a, B-31b, B-31c

A student paper sculpture is posed against a photograph of a tent-covered Mexican market place. The parallel, almost linear forms of paper structure and the series of suspended canvases that keep the hot sun from falling on the wares of the open-air market both clearly illustrate the enclosing of space through the use of several planes in conjunction. The way these planes can be arranged is infinitely varied and can create far-flung shapes or more compact structures like the student project.

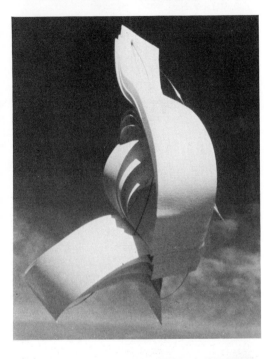

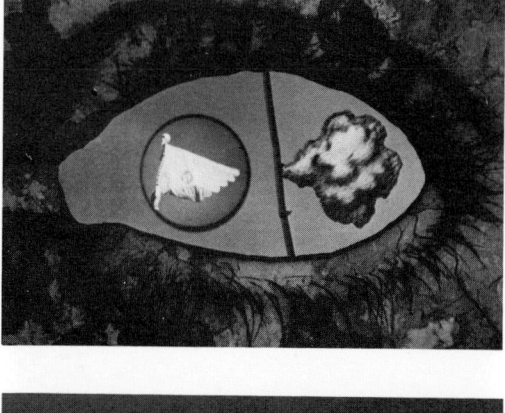

B&W B-32a, B-32b, B-32c

Two student works on the theme "World's End Parade Flag" illustrate planar form within the contemporary media of soft sculpture. The dollar bill on the top of a flagpole with a skull has been created from carved foam and cloth printed with the image of the money, which has been photostated up to a larger scale. The concept of automobile fumes polluting our world is carried to a logical expression in the stuffed canvas cloud of fumes coming from a tailpipe. From the point of view of visual form these flags combine planar and linear elements and represent a transition to linear three-dimensional form, which is the last and final stage of the continuum.

Aesthetically, modular paper sculptures by students demonstrate how a series of very open planar forms can define a mass that is impressive and powerful. Technically, these whimsical modules of Bristol board and Elmer's glue enable the artists to create very strong structures with an impressively small amount of material. The perforated sculpture on the right was about 20 inches high and encompassed a space measuring about 24 × 36 × 6 inches. If we were to weigh the piece, we would probably find we have less than eight ounces of paper.

We once assigned our students the problem of creating a paper planar enclosure strong enough to drop an egg about 90 feet from our third-floor classroom to the ground without breaking it. It was to be made of Bristol board, and measure no more than a foot square. From the evaluation point of view the experiment was a smashing success. In this project aesthetics were no longer the consideration, and the evaluation was done by the grim dictates of gravity. Great groans were heard as one egg after another broke, until halfway through the project a container flew through the air and fell to the ground with its cargo still intact. Of all the projects we taught in the design continuum, this one caused the least amount of controversy since failure and success were objectively determined.

B&W B-34a, B-34b, B-34c

Our last comparison of planar forms serves well to conclude our discussion of the use of a very thin plane to define and describe a major section of positive space. Another tropical leaf from Mexico is inset in a detail of a leaflike student project on painted Masonite. It is interesting to compare this deeply cut leaf with the broad plane of the leaf in B-30. Both describe a similar area of space, but the leaf shown here does its job with even less material. The plane of positive space has become whittled away to almost nothing, and what remains is a grouping of linear planes within the outline of a planar form.

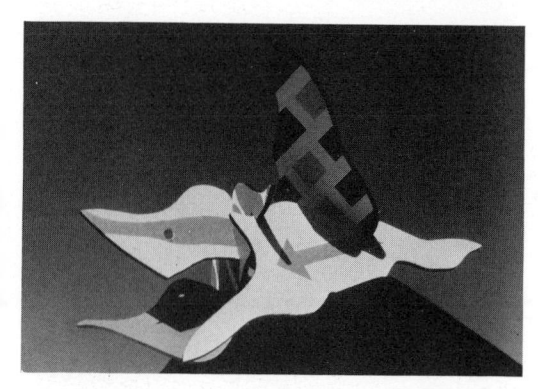

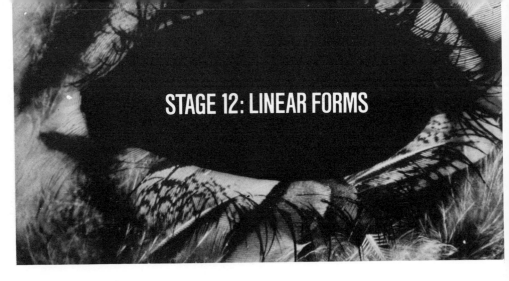

STAGE 12: LINEAR FORMS

CONCEPT

Linear forms create virtual volumes that suggest shapes in space by their outlines. What was once solid form in the earlier stages of the continuum has now become a skeleton of its former self, yet form can still be discerned clearly. The eye fills in the many spaces to complete the picture. Thus we can imagine the shape of a tree from the configuration of its bare branches in winter. Towering above us, these three-dimensional windows of line in space stand as a testament to the fortitude of mass in the face of imminent extinction. Now only a thin line separates mass from space.

At last we have come to the end of our evolutionary story, or is it just another beginning? Space has vanquished mass, eroded and pushed it into a corner. From the icy surface of the monolith, the textures, caves, and holes gave way to planes, and even these vestiges of mass dissipated into line in a reversal of the earliest part of the continuum. Now, gaunt and withdrawn, line, barely capable of even supporting itself, still supports the concept of form.

Stretching and bending, cutting corners and shooting straight out, line becomes the frenetic path of a point moving in space, trying to avoid in its frantic motion any further extinguishment. Then, like a puffy dandelion cast to the wind, lines break into dashes, dashes to dots, stars against the black night of infinite space. Our minds wander free of form, attracted here and there by a sense of brilliance, a flash of color, perhaps a shooting star or an airplane's signal strobe, until we come to rest on one and then another star. We begin to see a pattern, a constellation. If we connect one with another and then another we establish a geometric plane. Fill in the space and we produce that plane as a flat two-dimensional surface. Now what can we do with a flat two-dimensional surface? I wonder . . .

CONTEXT

Ladders and telephone poles, branches and bridges, steering wheels and wagon wheels, piano strings and shoestrings, radio aerials and TV antennas, pins and needles, fences and fingers—linear forms trace their fragile path across every space of our lives. *I'll drop you a line* said the fisherman as he cast about for his daily catch.

A skyrocket explodes across the Fourth of July, spewing fiery tracers out into flowers of rare temporal beauty. A tiny spider spins its web, catching in its fragile lines the dew and morning light. Power lines hang breathlessly across vast spaces, shaping architecture out of emptiness. Fields of grain spring sunward in waves of line. Pen and ink, drypoint and silver point, conté crayon and pastel—as artist and designers we can learn to create movement and music from drawing on the almost invisible resources of linear form.

APPROACHES AND MATERIALS

Spin a web of rope or string. Solder copper-coated rods into forms. Soak balsa-wood strips and bend them into wisps of linear music. Design a linear necklace, earrings, and wrist bracelet using thin wire. Solder it or bend and twist it around itself.

Create delicate chimes of hundreds of lines. Tie line to line with soft lines of string. Try tinsel and raffia, silk and jute, silver and nylon fishing line. Make a TV antenna for your own kind of signals. Tie up your telephone lines.

Find linear objects in stores and dumps and combine them into compositions. For ideas, study furniture made of linear materials like rattan and welded metal. Create square and round lines, long and short lines. For thick lines use dowels of wood, metal, and plastic, Plexiglas rod, and glass tubing. For thin lines use rubber bands, straws, toothpicks, matches, pencils, and paper clips.

Try to analyze a planar form with line, representing movement, density of space, expansion or contraction. Make an airplane wing, a tree branch, ladder-like forms.

CAPTION NOTES

The linear form uses an absolute minimum of positive space to describe a virtual volume it does not itself occupy. These elements play a most significant role, however, for without them, space has neither articulation nor form. They serve to structure space in the purest sense, creating sculptures out of the very air. Even without a knowledge of geometry it is clear to most people that the difference between a plane and a line is its relative width, and that a very long narrow plane approaches a linear form. Some of the examples in Stage 11 showed transitions like this. The only way in which the environment can play a greater part in the three-dimensional object is to obliterate it all together, reducing it once again to a series of lines on a flat surface. At this point we are back where we started from in the design continuum, at Stage 1.

It is difficult to conceive of the tie-in between linear three-dimensional forms and flat two-dimensional surfaces (Stages 12 to 1) unless one thinks of the tie-in between drawing in space with linear construction material and drawing on surfaces with pen or pencil. Then it is easy to link the beginning with the end.

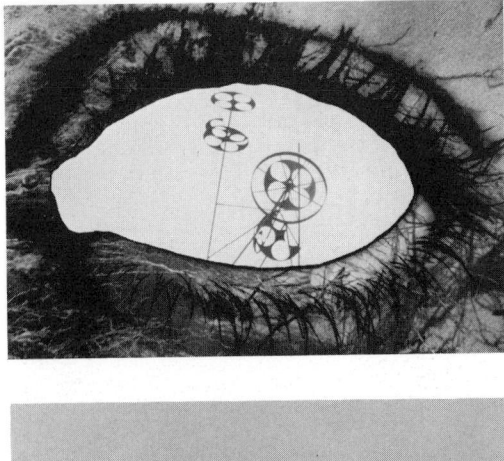

B&W B-35a, B-35b

A welded metal sculpture by a student makes a powerful statement about the last stage of our continuum. The circular areas clearly enclose the space within them, and we see the negative clover-leaf shape inside the circles as figure instead of ground. The holes which we began to see in penetrated masses now have become the shapes themselves.

In this last series of six images the Eye surround serves as a distinct contrast to the pieces. Instead of the airy blue sky as negative space, it is a solid mass of pitted and creviced ground on which the few wisps of dried grass and the eyelashes of our Eye draw their linear three-dimensional forms.

B&W B-36a, B-36b, B-36c

Two similar linear filigrees in space are juxtaposed here, and it is only when we look at the black-and-white illustrations that we see how different the pieces are. The background is a sculpture created by cutting circles of throw-away plastic cups (Styrofoam or plastic foam) and gluing them to one another to create a massed effect from essentially open modules. The center detail is from a roller-coaster framework. Although the amount of form is diminished compared to the magnitude of the space it describes, anyone who has ridden a roller coaster knows that this insubstantial-looking structure is a strong piece of functional architecture. Both of these pieces may help to put to rest some of the premises that we have put forth about the frailty of positive form in these last stages of the continuum, since both are structurally sound, as well as aesthetically powerful.

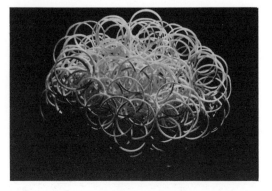

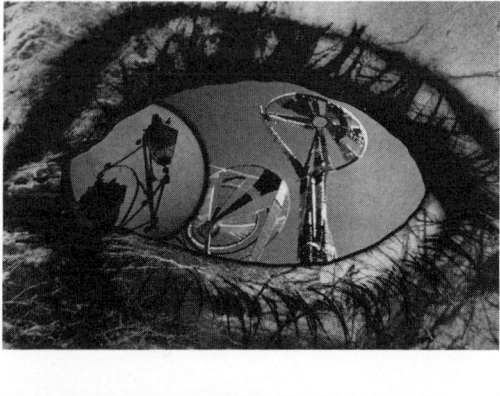

B&W B-37a, B-37b, B-37c

The play of light and shadow on these two linear structures is an essential element of their forms. The sculpture on the right is imaginatively composed of found floor-lamp bases and hoops that are joined and embellished with weaving and textured cloth. The black-and-white illustrations show the way in which value contrasts add to the effect of shadows falling on these thin structures, and seems to enhance its solidity. The inset on the left shows a street lamp casting a moody shadow on a wall in Guanajuato, Mexico. It is impossible to look at this lamp without seeing the shadow it creates as part of the form. Light itself can become an important part of the total design. With our new technology in photography and lasers, light sculptures are possible in which there is no material form at all, just space defined by value contrasts.

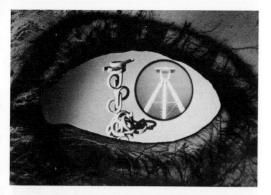

B&W B-38a, B-38b, B-38c

On the right, we are comparing a service station sign on Interstate 70 in Indiana to a student project created from a soldered copper pipe that has been rolled, formed, and painted. The service station sign, one of the many that visually pollute our countryside, thrusts up into space as a powerful linear monument when seen without the context of the environment. Part of the sense of power comes from the straightness of the lines On the other hand, the coiled pipes of the student work create linear convolutions that describe something close to a three-dimensional calligraphic drawing of a bird.

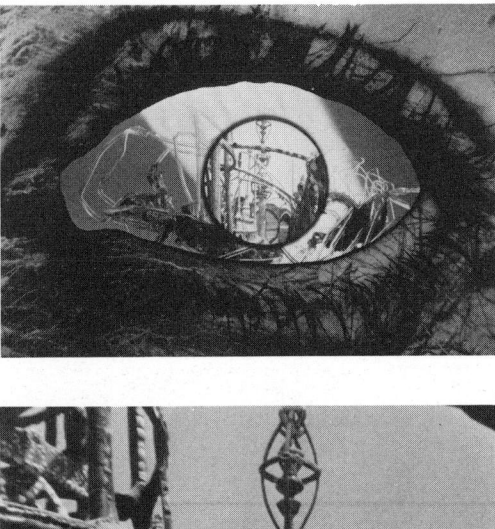

B&W B-39a, B-39b, B-39c

Here we have a visual analogy between architecture and sculpture. The inset detail is from the candy-cane filigree of the Watts Towers in Los Angeles. In Part 1 we used these unique monumental structures to illustrate the concept of how relief surfaces can be built up in a mosaic technique of found objects. There we mentioned that Simon Rodia created his Towers by himself, without helpers or commission. Like the works of Gaudi (B-26) to which they have been compared, the Watts Towers stand as a testament to how completely an artistic vision can be worked out in architecture. Rodia drew his vision in air with three-dimensional line.

The quality of the line that contributes to three-dimensional linear forms has varied a great deal in the preceding images. It can be delicate in scale (B-35) or massive (B-38), convoluted and massed (B-36), or created from open lines and curves (B-37). In this image we have contrasted an embellished linear element with the translucence of glass tubing in a heat-welded student sculpture. The student has effectively used these see-through lines in space to describe three-dimensional phenomena in their least solid appearance, where the light of the environment penetrates right through the positive form.

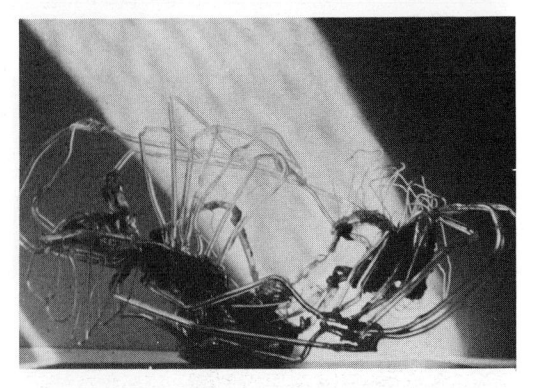

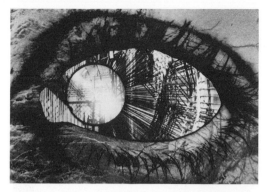

B&W B-40a, B-40b, B-40c

In this beautiful image that ends our design continuum, we have taken the liberty once again of enclosing a detail of a very large object within a detail of one much smaller in scale. In both, the barest minimum of linear three-dimensional form weaves in and out of space, creating a dense structure. Most interestingly, the piece at the left, which seems so ephemeral that light can weave in and out of it with more force than the basic material, is in reality part of a strong steel structure of the power station at Hoover Dam in Nevada. In the black-and-white illustration we can study the repeated interlacing and crisscrossing of very open linear forms. Such structures are seen so often in the countryside that we fail to pay attention to how wonderfully within them a minimal amount of positive space and a maximum amount of negative space perform their cooperative functions.

Compare this power station to the nonfunctional woven structure on a metal frame by a student. Here the interplay of positive and negative space is more compact, creating a functional strength that has been appreciated since primitive man first began to weave baskets. In details of woven structure, we have the very essence of linear form in which the scale of the object is often hard to determine, as you can see in the image. This detail might be of a chair seat or even of a suspension bridge.